Teach Yourself
VISUALLY™
Knitting

P9-DBY-486

Teach Yourself
VISUALLY™
Knitting

Visual

by Sharon Turner

WILEY

Wiley Publishing, Inc.

Teach Yourself VISUALLY™ Knitting

Copyright © 2006 by Wiley Publishing, Inc., Hoboken, New Jersey. All rights reserved.

Published by Wiley Publishing, Inc., Hoboken, New Jersey

No part of this publication may be reproduced, stored in a retrieval system or transmitted in any form or by any means, electronic, mechanical, photocopying, recording, scanning or otherwise, except as permitted under Sections 107 or 108 of the 1976 United States Copyright Act, without either the prior written permission of the Publisher, or authorization through payment of the appropriate per-copy fee to the Copyright Clearance Center, 222 Rosewood Drive, Danvers, MA 01923, (978) 750-8400, fax (978) 646-8600, or on the web at www.copyright.com. Requests to the Publisher for permission should be addressed to the Legal Department, Wiley Publishing, Inc., 10475 Crosspoint Blvd., Indianapolis, IN 46256, (317) 572-3447, fax (317) 572-4355, or online at http://www.wiley.com/go/permissions.

Wiley, the Wiley Publishing logo, Teach Yourself VISUALLY, and related trademarks are trademarks or registered trademarks of John Wiley & Sons, Inc. and/or its affiliates. All other trademarks are the property of their respective owners. Wiley Publishing, Inc. is not associated with any product or vendor mentioned in this book.

The publisher and the author make no representations or warranties with respect to the accuracy or completeness of the contents of this work and specifically disclaim all warranties, including without limitation warranties of fitness for a particular purpose. No warranty may be created or extended by sales or promotional materials. The advice and strategies contained herein may not be suitable for every situation. This work is sold with the understanding that the publisher is not engaged in rendering legal, accounting, or other professional services. If professional assistance is required, the services of a competent professional person should be sought. Neither the publisher nor the author shall be liable for damages arising here from. The fact that an organization or Website is referred to in this work as a citation and/or a potential source of further information does not mean that the author or the publisher endorses the information the organization or Website may provide or recommendations it may make. Further, readers should be aware that Internet Websites listed in this work may have changed or disappeared between when this work was written and when it is read.

For general information on our other products and services or to obtain technical support please contact our Customer Care Department within the U.S. at (800) 762-2974, outside the U.S. at (317) 572-3993 or fax (317) 572-4002.

Wiley also publishes its books in a variety of electronic formats. Some content that appears in print may not be available in electronic books. For more information about Wiley products, please visit our web site at www.wiley.com.

Library of Congress Control Number: 2005024428

ISBN-13: 978-0-7645-9640-7

ISBN-10: 0-7645-9640-3

Printed in the United States of America

10   9   8   7   6   5

Book production by Wiley Publishing, Inc. Composition Services

Praise for the Teach Yourself VISUALLY Series

I just had to let you and your company know how great I think your books are. I just purchased my third Visual book (my first two are dog-eared now!) and, once again, your product has surpassed my expectations. The expertise, thought, and effort that go into each book are obvious, and I sincerely appreciate your efforts. Keep up the wonderful work!

—Tracey Moore (Memphis, TN)

I have several books from the Visual series and have always found them to be valuable resources.

—Stephen P. Miller (Ballston Spa, NY)

Thank you for the wonderful books you produce. It wasn't until I was an adult that I discovered how I learn—visually. Although a few publishers out there claim to present the material visually, nothing compares to Visual books. I love the simple layout. Everything is easy to follow. And I understand the material! You really know the way I think and learn. Thanks so much!

—Stacey Han (Avondale, AZ)

Like a lot of other people, I understand things best when I see them visually. Your books really make learning easy and life more fun.

—John T. Frey (Cadillac, MI)

I am an avid fan of your Visual books. If I need to learn anything, I just buy one of your books and learn the topic in no time. Wonders! I have even trained my friends to give me Visual books as gifts.

—Illona Bergstrom (Aventura, FL)

I write to extend my thanks and appreciation for your books. They are clear, easy to follow, and straight to the point. Keep up the good work! I bought several of your books and they are just right! No regrets! I will always buy your books because they are the best.

—Seward Kollie (Dakar, Senegal)

Credits

Acquisitions Editor
Pam Mourouzis

Project Editor
Kitty Wilson Jarrett

Technical Editor
Penny Little

Editorial Manager
Christina Stambaugh

Publisher
Cindy Kitchel

Vice President and Executive Publisher
Kathy Nebenhaus

Interior Design
Kathie Rickard
Elizabeth Brooks

Cover Design
José Almaguer

Cover and Interior Photography
Matt Bowen

Special Thanks...

To the following companies for providing the yarn for the projects shown in this book:

- elann.com (www.elann.com)
- Muench Yarns (www.muenchyarns.com)
- Cascade Yarns (www.cascadeyarns.com)
- Dale of Norway Yarns (www.daleofnorway.com)
- Plymouth Yarn Company (www.plymouthyarn.com)
- S.R. Kertzer Yarns (www.kertzer.com)

About the Author

Sharon Turner designs knitwear and publishes a line of knitting patterns under the trademark Monkeysuits. She is the author of *Monkeysuits: Sweaters and More to Knit for Kids.* Sharon lives in Brooklyn, New York, with her husband and three daughters.

Acknowledgments

Thank you always to my dear family. For helping with the knitting, many, many thanks go to Doll, Sue Paul, Cindy Kitchel, Kristen Balouch, and Jill Draper. Ann Cannon-Brown, of elann.com, provided many skeins of her beautiful Peruvian Collection Highland Wool for most of the swatches and was willing to give much more. Thank you also to Kirstin Muench, of Muench Yarns, for the constant supply of exciting yarns. Finally, Pam Mourouzis, Kitty Jarrett, Cindy Kitchel, and Christina Stambaugh worked so hard and contributed so much that this is really their book, too.

Table of Contents

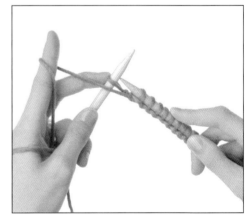

 **chapter 3** Basic Stitch Patterns 32

 **chapter 4** Shaping 46

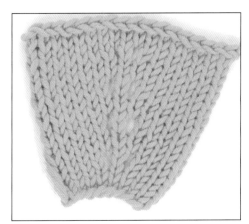

chapter 5 Correcting Mistakes 64

chapter 6 Learning to Read Written Instructions 74

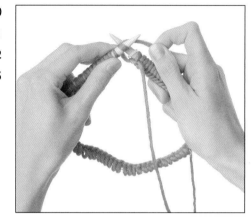

chapter 8 **More Complicated Stitch Patterns: Bobbles, Knots, and Cables   94**

chapter **9** Openwork 106

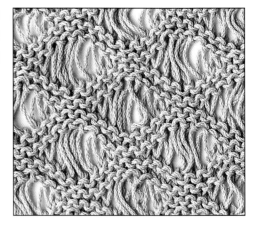

chapter **10** Color Knitting 114

chapter 11   Finishing Techniques   134

chapter 12   Finishing Details   150

chapter 13 Decorative Details 174

chapter 14 Easy Knitting Projects 200

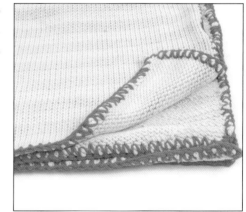

chapter 17 **Happy Endings** **262**

chapter 1

Introduction to Knitting

Are you ready to learn how to knit? Before you put any stitches on a needle, you need to do some initial preparation. There are so many choices in terms of knitting yarns and tools that it's a good idea to get to know what's available and what you need before you start.

Get yourself some yarn and needles and let this book walk you through the basics of knitting. By the end of the first few chapters, you will be proficient enough to create a beautiful scarf, a bag, or even a hat.

Once you begin to get into a knitting rhythm, you'll discover one of the most relaxing and satisfying of hobbies. Sitting down and taking up your knitting—the feel of soft, warm wool running through your fingers, the look of vivid color against color, the excitement of watching your fabric grow—will become one of the highlights of your day.

Grandmothers are not the only ones who have discovered the joy of knitting. Knitting has grown so much in popularity over the past decade that there are knitting groups, knitting Web sites, and pattern books geared toward knitters of all ages and sensibilities. Children and teens are knitting in after-school groups, twenty-somethings are holding knitting circles in cafes, and new mothers are celebrating the births of their babies by knitting for them.

As more people have taken up knitting, the selection of yarns and tools has grown by leaps and bounds. Walk into any yarn shop, and the riot of texture and color will overwhelm and entice you. You'll discover what seasoned knitters mean when they talk about the tremendous "stashes" of yarn hidden under their beds and in their closets.

What's also wonderful about knitting is that you can take it with you everywhere. You may even begin to look forward to time spent in the doctor's waiting room, or at your daughter's violin lesson, or on a long train ride. You won't be able to leave for vacation until you have packed a selection of knitting projects.

A hand-knit gift has extra meaning for both the person giving and the one receiving. When you knit a special hat, scarf, or baby sweater for someone, you weave your love into the fabric, and the person receiving your gift will know it and appreciate it.

It's no wonder that people have been knitting for centuries. Even now, when sweaters can be mass-produced by machine, people are still choosing to create by hand. Hand knitting is a creative outlet that satisfies the senses and soothes the nerves. It's good for you. Did you know that the rhythmic repetition of hand knitting can induce brain waves similar to those achieved through meditation? Once you learn the basic techniques that follow—and they're easy— you, too, can let your needles fly and your mind wander.

Knitting yarns come in so many fibers, weights, and textures that you may be overwhelmed when you first walk into a yarn shop. You can use the guide that follows to help choose yarns.

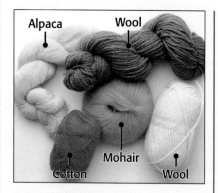

NATURAL FIBERS

Many knitters choose yarns spun from animal fibers, like wool, alpaca, mohair, cashmere, and angora, because they are generally the warmest to wear and hold their shape well. *Wool* comes in a range of textures, from sometimes scratchy Shetlands to softer merinos. *Alpaca* is a luxuriously soft fiber that has a lot of drape. *Mohair* is hairier than wool, and mohair-only garments have a fuzzy halo. *Cashmere* comes from goats and is the softest and most expensive fiber. *Angora,* which is spun from rabbits, is also extremely soft and fuzzy. *Silk* is also warm, but it's not as elastic as wool. Garments made from *cotton* and *linen* yarns are generally lighter and good for warm weather wear. These yarns, however, are heavier and less elastic than wool. Large sweaters knit in heavy cotton tend to lose their shape over time.

SYNTHETIC FIBERS

Synthetics include *acrylic, nylon,* and *polyester.* These yarns are human-made and often less expensive than natural fibers. Many are machine-washable.

BLENDS

Two or more fibers can be combined and spun into one yarn; these yarns are called *blends.* The combinations are limitless, and certain characteristics of a fiber can be altered by combining it with another fiber. For example, cotton can be improved in body and elasticity by being combined with acrylic; combining wool with alpaca or cashmere can soften it.

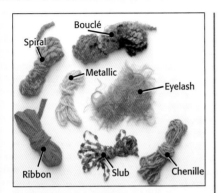

NOVELTY YARNS

Furry, metallic, and bumpy yarns are called *novelty yarns*. These yarns work well for trims and dressy garments, and they can be doubled with another yarn for added texture and color. Novelty yarns are not recommended for beginners, as it is difficult to see stitches and mistakes in a fabric knit in novelty yarn.

Fingering

Sport

Double knitting

Worsted weight

Bulky

Super bulky

YARN WEIGHTS

Yarn weight refers to the thickness of a yarn. There are essentially five weights: fingering or baby, sport, double knitting (DK), worsted weight, and bulky. You will probably come across variations within these categories as well, such as lace weight, light worsted, Aran weight, heavy worsted, and super bulky.

BALLS, SKEINS, AND HANKS

Yarn comes packaged in many shapes. Yarn can come in a *ball*, with a label in the center, or as a *skein*, with the label wrapped around the middle. Both balls and skeins can be knit from directly. Some yarns come in *hanks*, which look like twisted braids. You must wind a hank into a ball before using it, or it will become tangled.

Most yarns come packaged with a label, also called a *ball band*. Always save your ball band with your yarn, as it contains useful information regarding the yarn.

The largest print on the ball band is the yarn manufacturer's name and/or logo, and then the name of that particular yarn. Also included is the fiber content of the yarn.

The ball band also lists the weight of the ball and the yardage, or the length of yarn contained in the ball. Yarn companies assign numbers to indicate color. These numbers are not the same from one manufacturer to the next. Also listed is a *dye lot* number. Yarns are dyed in large batches, or lots, and the dye lot number refers to a particular batch of a particular color. It's important to buy enough yarn from the same dye lot for a project because color differs from one dye lot to the next.

The yarn label also lists what size knitting needles to use with the yarn and what the desired gauge is for that yarn when knit with those needles. Care instructions are usually shown in the form of symbols like those found on clothing labels.

Weight 100g/220 yards

Needle size:
7 = 5 st per 1î
8 = 4½ st per 1"

Col. no. 32
Lot no. 1077

fine wool yarns
Soft & Thick
Made in the U.S.A.

90% Merino Wool
5% Alpaca
5% Cashmere

ᵀᴹ

fine wool

It is a good idea to become familiar with the symbols used to indicate care instructions for a particular yarn. You need to know this information when it comes time to clean your hand-knit item.

Symbols using the image of a tub or washing machine indicate whether a fiber is machine- or hand-washable. Note that the symbol of the tub with an X over it means the fiber is neither machine- nor hand-washable. The triangular symbols indicate bleaching instructions.

Symbols using the image of an iron indicate whether a fiber can be pressed. The symbol of the iron with dots in it illustrates what temperature should be used when pressing.

Circular symbols illustrate dry-cleaning instructions. If the circle has an X through it, the fiber should not be dry-cleaned. Circles with letters in them indicate what chemicals should be used to dry-clean the fiber. The people at your dry-cleaner should be able to tell you what solvents they use.

MACHINE WASH TEMPERATURE	BLEACH	IRON TEMPERATURE (Dry or Steam)	DRY-CLEAN TEMPERATURE
Do Not Wash	Do Not Bleach	Do Not Iron	Do Not Dry-Clean
Hand Wash	Any Bleach (when needed)	Low	Dry-Clean, Petroleum Solvent Only (F)
Normal		Medium	Dry-Clean, Any Solvent Except Trichloroethylene (P)
Delicate/Gentle		High	Dry-Clean, Any Solvent (A)
Cool/Cold			
Warm			
Hot			

Knitting needles come in many shapes and sizes, and they are made from several different materials. Try out various types to see which ones work best for you. There are also a number of accessories on the market, but you will only need a few to start. As you complete more and more projects, your collection of needles and accessories will gradually expand.

TYPES OF NEEDLES

Knitting needles come in metal, plastic, wood, and bamboo. Yarn slides easily along metal. Plastic needles are lightweight but can bend. Wood needles are beautiful and can be more expensive than metal or plastic. Bamboo needles are lighter and less expensive than wood needles. Some teachers recommend bamboo for beginners because the surface slows yarn from slipping off the needle.

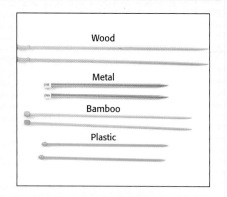

SIZES OF NEEDLES

Needle sizing can be confusing because one needle has three numbers indicating the size. Most important is the diameter of the needle shaft, measured in millimeters (mm). A U.S. numbering system ranging from 0 for the thinnest needle to 50 for the thickest needle also labels size. Also listed on a needle is a UK/Canadian number ranging from 14 for the thinnest needle to 000 for the thickest needle. A needle's shaft length is measured in inches, and this number also generally appears on a needle or needle package. The UK/Canadian numbering system differs from the U.S. system, so it's better to buy needles based on diameter than on numbering system. The chart below shows needle size in metric as well as both U.S. and UK/Canadian numbering.

Needle Sizes		
Metric (mm)	U.S.	UK/Canadian
2.0	0	14
2.25–2.5	1	13
2.75	2	12
3.0	–	11
3.25	3	10
3.5	4	–
3.75	5	9
4.0	6	8
4.5	7	7
5.0	8	6
5.5	9	5
6.0	10	4

Metric (mm)	U.S.	UK/Canadian
6.5	10½	3
7.0	10¾	2
7.5	–	1
8.0	11	0
9.0	13	00
10.0	15	000
12.0–12.75	17	–
16.0	19	–
19.0	35	–
20.0	36	–
25.0	50	–

SHAPES OF NEEDLES

Knitting needles come in three shapes. *Straight needles,* also called single-point needles, come in various lengths and have a point on one end and a knob on the other. *Double-pointed needles,* pointed on both ends, are sold in sets of four or five. *Circular needles,* which have two points connected by a nylon cord, come in a variety of lengths and materials.

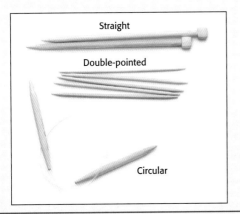

Straight

Double-pointed

Circular

ESSENTIAL ACCESSORIES

You need to equip yourself with a small pair of *scissors* and a *tape measure. Row counters* record rows knit. *Tapestry needles* are used for sewing knit pieces together and darning in loose ends. *Point protectors* prevent work from slipping off the needles. A *stitch and needle gauge* measures not only stitch and row gauge but also needle diameter.

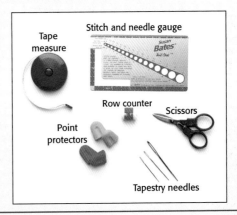

Stitch and needle gauge

Tape measure

Row counter

Scissors

Point protectors

Tapestry needles

OTHER ACCESSORIES

Stitch holders hold stitches to be worked later. Plastic-headed *knitting pins* fasten knit pieces together before sewing. *Stitch markers* are small plastic rings used to mark a point in knitting where an increase, a decrease, or a pattern change occurs. *Cable needles* come in several styles and are used to hold stitches when making knit cables.

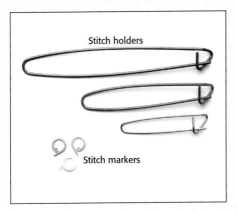

Stitch holders

Stitch markers

HANDY EXTRAS

You may want to get a *knitting bag*: Choose one that stands open, has a smooth interior, and has some pockets for accessories. Small amounts of yarn are wound on plastic *bobbins,* useful for some types of color knitting. *Crochet hooks* come in handy for making edgings and ties. *Pompom makers* are great for making thick, round pompoms.

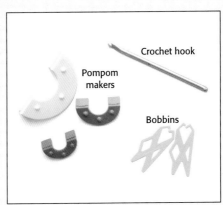

Crochet hook

Pompom makers

Bobbins

chapter 2

Basic Techniques

A knit fabric is made up of many tiny knit stitches. In this chapter, you will learn the basics: how to get your first row of stitches on the needle as well as how to knit and purl those stitches, using a variety of methods. Once you're able to knit and purl, there is no end to what you can create. After you master knit and purl stitches, you will learn how to join new yarn, so that you won't have to stop when your yarn runs out. Finally, you will find out how to bind off, which is what you do to remove your stitches from the needle when you're done.

Make a Slipknot

The time has come to pick up your needles and learn to knit. You need a ball of worsted weight or bulky yarn and a pair of needles in the size that the yarn's ball band calls for. When you have those things, you are ready to put your very first stitch—a *slipknot*—onto your needle. You have probably made a slipknot before, but there's a special method for putting one onto your knitting needle.

How to Make a Slipknot

① Starting about 10 inches in from the end of your yarn, make a loop.

② Pull the working yarn (the yarn coming from the ball) behind the loop as shown. Insert the needle underneath the working yarn and pull it up through the loop.

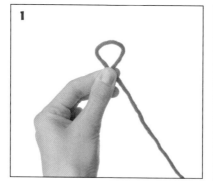

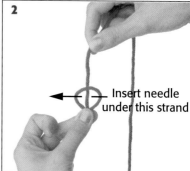

Insert needle under this strand

③ Pull the ends of the yarn so that the slipknot sits snugly on the needle.

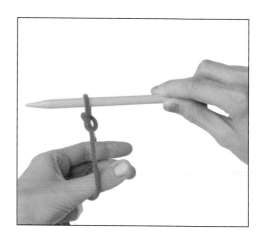

Cast On: Simple Cast-On

Casting on is what you do to get a foundation row of stitches on your needle so that you can start to knit. There are many cast-on methods, each with different results.

This method of casting on is the easiest and quickest, so it's good for beginners. It does not, however, create the neatest edge.

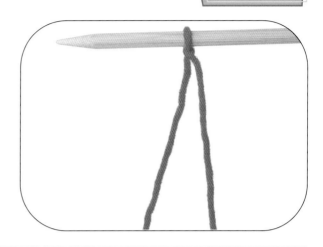

Simple Cast-On

1. With the needle with the slipknot on it in your right hand and the working yarn in your left, make a loop with the working yarn.

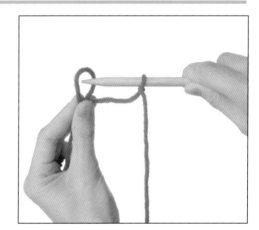

2. Place the loop onto the needle with your left hand and then pull the working yarn to tighten.

3. Repeat steps 1 and 2 until you have the desired number of stitches on the needle.

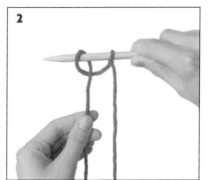

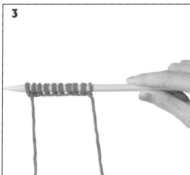

Cast On: Long-Tail Cast-On

You may think that this method of casting on stitches looks complicated, but once you master it, it's very quick and easy. This method also provides a neat, elastic edge. Take care not to cast on too tightly, or your edge will have no elasticity. You might want to cast on to a needle a size or two larger than the size you should use for the project; then, when you begin knitting, you switch to the correct size.

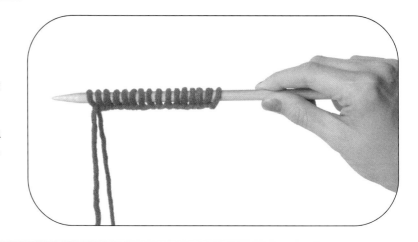

Long-Tail Cast-On

① Put a slipknot on your needle, leaving a tail that's the equivalent of 1 inch per stitch you plan to cast on, plus a few more inches. (So if you plan to cast on 12 stitches, leave a tail that's about 15 inches long.)

② Hold the yarn with the tail wrapped over your thumb and the working yarn over your forefinger, grasping both ends with your pinky and ring finger in the center of your palm.

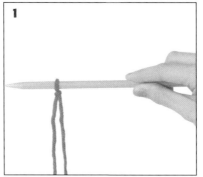

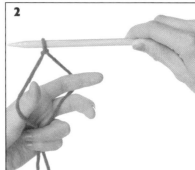

③ Lower the needle to create a V while holding the slipknot in place with your right forefinger.

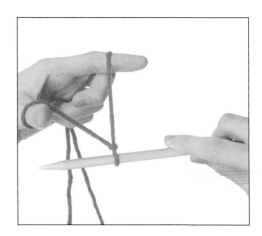

4 Insert the needle up and under the yarn that is looped around the outside of your thumb.

5 Move the needle to the right and use it to grab the yarn from the nearest side of your forefinger (a); then pull it through the loop between your thumb and the needle (b).

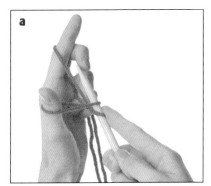

a

b

6 Once the yarn is pulled through the loop between your thumb and needle, drop the loops from your thumb and forefinger and pull both ends of the yarn to tighten the stitch on the needle.

You have just cast on 1 stitch.

7 Repeat steps 2–6 until you have cast on the desired number of stitches.

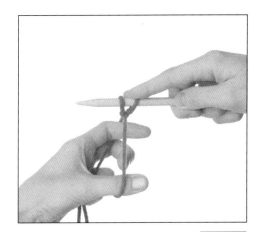

Hold Needles and Yarn

Some people knit holding the yarn in their right hand, which is called the *English method*, while others hold it in their left hand, which is called the *Continental method*. Try both methods and experiment to see which suits you. The most important thing is to be relaxed and comfortable.

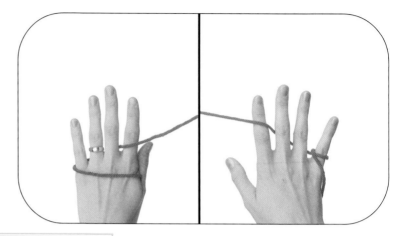

Holding Needles and Yarn for the English Method

1 Holding the needle with the stitches on it in your left hand, wind the working yarn in a loop around your pinky, under your two middle fingers, and over the forefinger of your right hand.

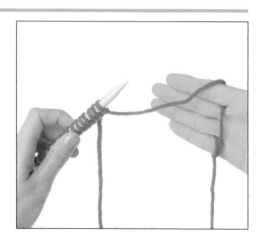

2 Hold the empty needle (called the working needle) in your right hand while keeping the working yarn wound through your fingers to maintain even tension.

Holding Needles and Yarn for the Continental Method

1 Holding the needle with the stitches on it in your right hand, wind the working yarn around the back of your hand, under your pinky and two middle fingers, and over the forefinger of your left hand.

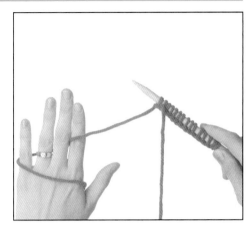

2 Take the needle with the stitches on it back into your left hand, keeping the working yarn wound through your fingers to maintain even tension, and hold the working (empty) needle in your right hand.

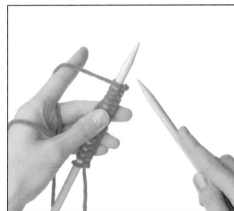

FAQ

When I wind the yarn around my fingers as described, it feels loose and awkward. Is there another way to hold the yarn?

Yes, there are infinite ways. If it feels too loose, or if wrapping the yarn around your pinky is awkward, try wrapping the yarn over your palm instead. The important thing is to be comfortable and to have the yarn flow easily through your fingers. Many knitters make up their own way of holding the yarn.

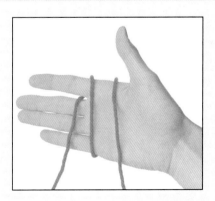

Knit: English Method

Now that you know how to cast on stitches and hold your yarn and needles, you can try actually knitting. Many Americans use the English method—holding the yarn with the right hand—but you don't have to be right-handed to use this method.

It's a good idea to start with a small number of stitches (10–15) on your needles. You will want to count your stitches after every row to make sure you haven't dropped or added any accidentally.

How to Knit Using the English Method

① Hold the needle with the cast-on stitches on it in your left hand and hold the working (empty) needle in your right hand, with the working yarn wound around the fingers of your right hand.

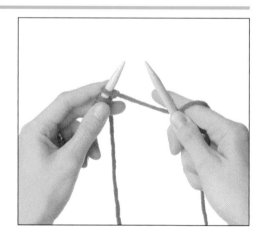

② Holding the yarn in back of both needles, insert the right needle into the front of the first stitch on the left needle.

Your needles will form an X, with the right needle behind the left needle.

③ Holding the crossed needles between your left thumb and forefinger, bring the working yarn around the right needle from back to front (a) and then bring it down between the two needles (b).

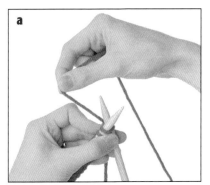

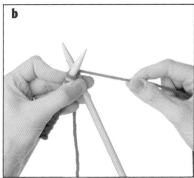

④ Pull the right needle toward the front, bringing the new loop of yarn you just wrapped around it through the cast-on stitch (a), and slip the cast-on stitch off the left needle (b).

You now have 1 stitch on the right needle–your first knit stitch.

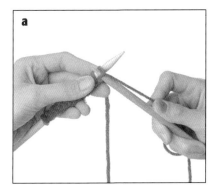

⑤ Repeat steps 2–4 for each remaining cast-on stitch, until all the new stitches are on the right needle.

When you have knit all the stitches from the left needle, you have completed one *row* of knitting.

⑥ Switch the needle with the stitches on it to your left hand and repeat steps 2–5 for each row.

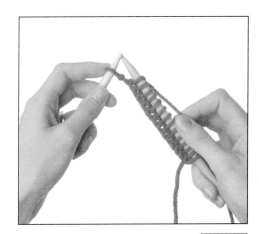

Knit: Continental Method

Now you can try knitting using the Continental method, in which you hold the yarn and control tension with your left hand. Don't worry if you're right-handed, though: Both right-handed and left-handed Europeans have been knitting this way for centuries.

How to Knit Using the Continental Method

1 Hold the needle with the cast-on stitches on it in your left hand and hold the working (empty) needle in your right hand, with the working yarn wound around the fingers of your left hand.

2 Insert the right needle into the front of the first stitch on the left needle, holding the yarn in back of both needles.

Your needles will form an X, with the right needle behind the left needle.

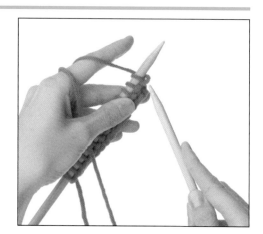

3 Use your left forefinger to wrap yarn around the right needle from front to back.

Note: This is a small, quick motion involving primarily the left forefinger. You can help it along by grabbing the yarn with the right needle at the same time.

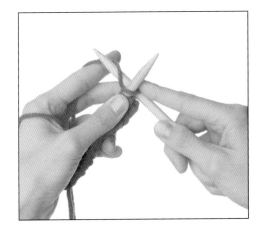

4 Pull the right needle toward the front, bringing the new loop of yarn you just wrapped around it through the cast-on stitch (a), and slip the cast-on stitch off the left needle (b).

You now have 1 stitch on the right needle—your first knit stitch.

Note: You may want to use your right forefinger to keep the wrapped strand from slipping off the tip of the needle at step 4 (a).

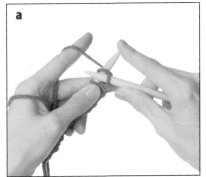

5 Repeat steps 2–4 for each remaining cast-on stitch, until all the new stitches are on the right needle.

When you have knit all the stitches from the left needle, you have completed one *row* of knitting.

6 Switch the needle with the stitches on it to your left hand and repeat steps 2–5 for each row.

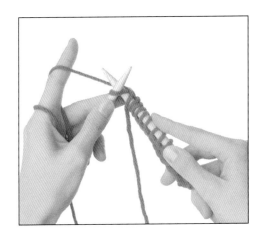

Purl: English Method

When you have mastered the knit stitch, you are ready to try the *purl* stitch. Purling is the opposite of knitting. You hold the needles the same way as for knitting, but you keep the yarn in front of the needles instead of at the back.

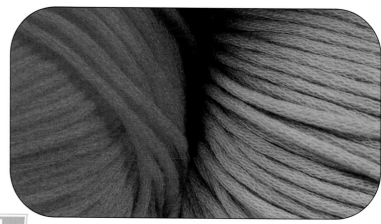

How to Purl Using the English Method

1 Hold the needle with the cast-on stitches on it in your left hand and hold both the working (empty) needle and the working yarn in your right hand.

2 Holding the yarn in front of both needles, insert the right needle from back to front (that is, from right to left) into the first stitch on the left needle.

Your needles will form an X, with the right needle in front of the left needle.

3 Hold the crossed needles between your left thumb and forefinger and bring the yarn behind the right needle, or between the crossed needles (a); then wrap the yarn around the right needle in a counterclockwise direction (b).

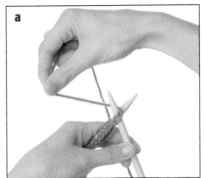
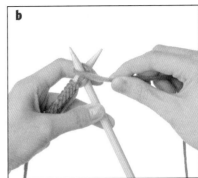

4 Pull the right needle toward the back, bringing the new loop of yarn you just wrapped around it through the cast-on stitch (a); then slip the cast-on stitch off the left needle (b).

You now have 1 stitch on the right needle—your first purl stitch.

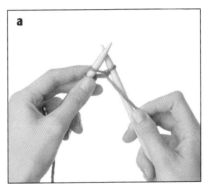
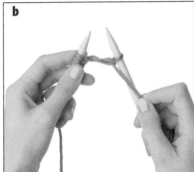

5 Repeat steps 2–4 for each remaining cast-on stitch, until all the new stitches are on the right needle.

When you have purled all the stitches from the left needle, you have completed one *row* of purling.

6 Switch the needle with stitches on it back to your left hand and repeat steps 2–5 for each row.

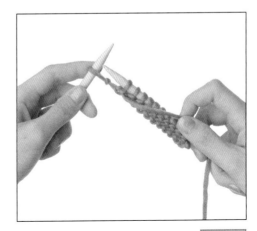

Purl: Continental Method

When you purl using the Continental method, you not only hold the yarn and control tension with your left hand but also hold the yarn in front of the needles, as for the English method.

The Continental method makes it easier to move the yarn from the front of the needles to the back of the needles in the same row. When you begin to mix knitting and purling in the same row, as for ribbing or other combination stitches, you really see the difference.

How to Purl Using the Continental Method

① Hold the needle with the cast-on stitches on it in your left hand and hold the working (empty) needle in your right hand, with the working yarn wound around the fingers of your left hand.

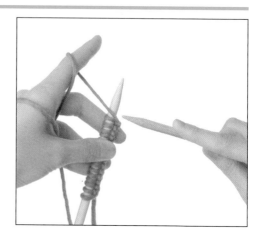

② Holding the yarn in front of both needles, insert the right needle from back to front (that is, from right to left) into the first stitch on the left needle.

The needles will form an X, with the right needle in front of the left needle.

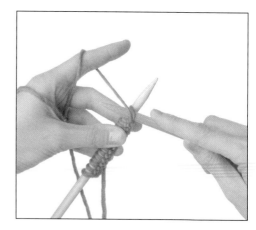

3 Use your left forefinger to wrap the yarn around the right needle from front to back, between the needles, and back to the front of the right needle.

Note: This is a small, quick motion involving flicking your left forefinger down, bringing the yarn between the needles and then back up, and creating a loop on the right needle.

4 Pull the right needle toward the back, bringing the new loop of yarn you just wrapped around it through the cast-on stitch (a); then slip the cast-on stitch off the left needle (b).

You now have 1 stitch on the right needle– your first purl stitch.

Note: You may want to use your right forefinger to keep the wrapped strand from slipping off the tip of the needle at step 4 (a).

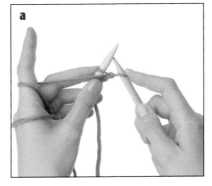

5 Repeat steps 2–4 for each remaining cast-on stitch, until all the new stitches are on the right needle.

When you have purled all the stitches from the left needle, you have completed one *row* of purling.

6 Switch the needle with stitches on it back to your left hand and repeat steps 2–5 for each row.

Join New Yarn

Have you run out of yarn yet? If not, there will come a time when you run out or want to change color. At that time, you'll need to know how to join a new ball of yarn.

How to Join New Yarn

AT THE BEGINNING OF A ROW

It's better to join a new ball at the beginning of a row than in the middle. That way, you can sew your loose ends into a seam or an edge. When your first ball of yarn has length remaining that is less than four times the width of your knitting, it's time to change to a new ball. At that point, finish your row and cut off the old yarn, leaving a 6-inch tail.

1 Tie a 6-inch end from your new ball snugly onto the tail of the old yarn.

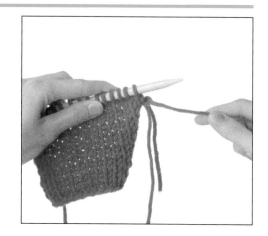

2 Taking care not to confuse the new working yarn with the tied end, work across the row as usual.

Note: When you finish your project, you can untie the knot and weave in the ends to hide them.

IN THE MIDDLE OF A ROW

Sometimes you have no choice but to join a new yarn in the middle of a row. If you're knitting in the round, or if you're working on a color pattern that changes in the middle of a row, for example, this is what you have to do. Make sure you have at least 6 inches of the old yarn left to weave in later.

1 Work the next stitch using the new yarn; knit if it should be a knit stitch or purl if it should be a purl stitch.

2 After you complete the row, tie the two ends together somewhat loosely so that they don't become unraveled.

Note: When you finish your project, you can untie the knot and weave in the ends to hide them.

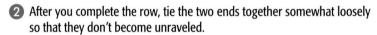
How to Splice New Yarn

Splicing works only with yarn that is the same color and that has more than one ply (that is, is made up of more than one strand of fiber twisted together). It works well for joins in the middle of a row and has the advantage of not creating a bumpy knot in the back; it has the disadvantage of taking some skill to master.

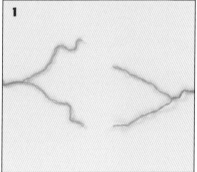

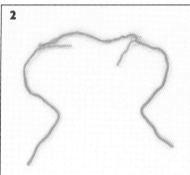

1 Untwist the ends of the old yarn and the new yarn for 3 to 4 inches and separate the plies into two clumps for each yarn.

2 Twist one clump of strands from the old yarn together with one clump of strands from the new yarn. Continue working the row as usual with the new yarn.

Note: You can weave in the loose plies later.

Bind Off

Binding off is what you do when you want to get your stitches off the needle permanently, without allowing them to unravel. You may bind off at the very end of a project to finish it, or you may shape your garment's armholes or neck by binding off a few stitches here and there. New knitters often bind off so tightly that the finished edge has no elasticity. If your bound-off edge seems too tight, try using a larger needle to bind off.

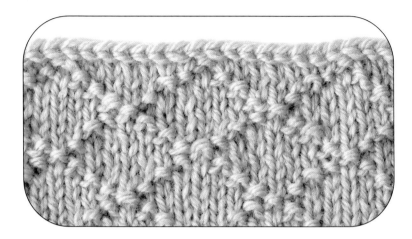

How to Bind Off Knitwise

This method is the most frequently used, and it is the easiest bind-off. You use it to bind off knit stitches. Remember to keep it loose.

1. Knit until you have 2 stitches total on the right needle; then insert the left needle into the front of the first stitch knit onto the right needle.

2. Pull the first stitch over the second knit stitch and off the right needle.

   You have bound off 1 stitch *knitwise,* and you have 1 stitch on the right needle.

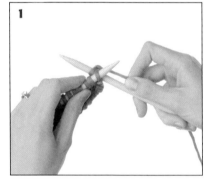

3. Repeat steps 1 and 2 until you have bound off the desired number of stitches.

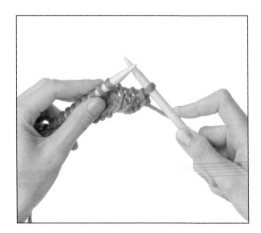

How to Bind Off Purlwise

This method is just like the knit bind-off, except you purl instead of knit. You use it to bind off purl stitches.

1. Purl until you have 2 stitches total on the right needle; then insert the left needle into the front of the first stitch purled onto the right needle.

2. Pull the first stitch over the second purled stitch and off the right needle.

   You have bound off 1 stitch *purlwise,* and you have 1 stitch on the right needle.

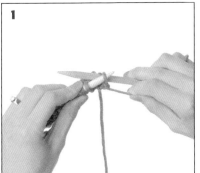

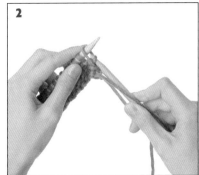

3. Repeat steps 1 and 2 until you have bound off the desired number of stitches.

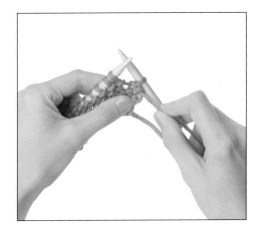

FAQ

What do I do when I have bound off all stitches and have only 1 left on the right needle?

When you are binding off all the stitches that remain and you have only 1 stitch remaining on the right needle, cut your working yarn, leaving a tail at least 6 inches long. Thread this tail through the last stitch and pull tight.

chapter 3

Basic Stitch Patterns

Now that you have accomplished knitting and purling, you're ready to move on to learning some basic stitch patterns. You can create infinite patterns using just knit and purl stitches. Very simple stitch repeats can result in highly textured designs. Take some time to experiment.

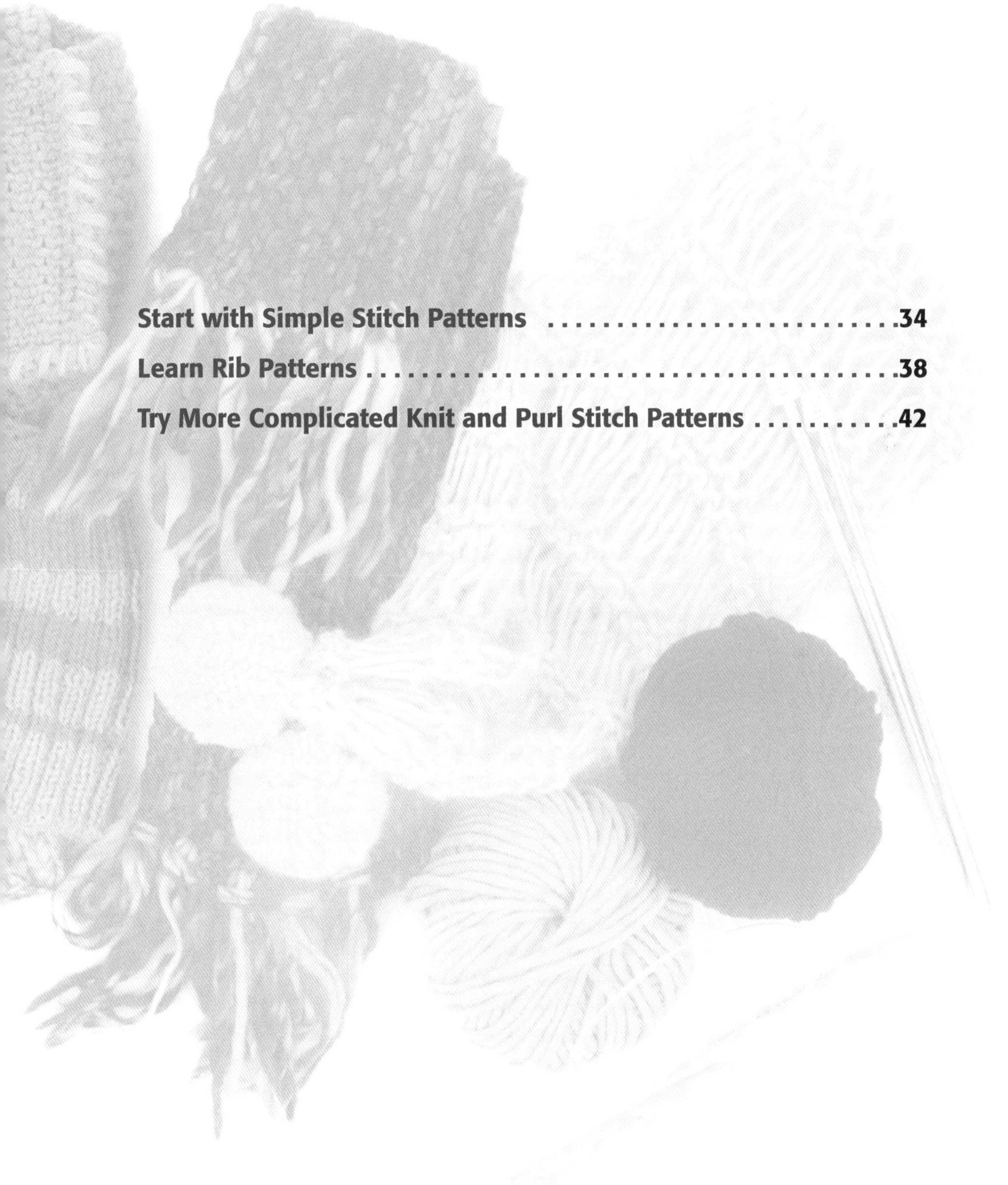

Start with Simple Stitch Patterns

Here are a few basic stitch patterns that you can try. For some of them, you knit or purl different rows, and for others, you knit and purl in the same row. Many of these patterns are good for allover designs as well as for edgings and borders. Learning new stitch patterns will improve your ability to recognize which stitch is a knit and which stitch is a purl.

Simple Stitch Patterns

GARTER STITCH

Garter stitch is the easiest stitch pattern, and what's great about it is that it always lies perfectly flat. It looks exactly the same on both the front and the back.

1. Row 1: Knit.
2. Repeat row 1 for garter stitch.

   After you knit several rows, you see horizontal ridges appear. Two knit rows form one ridge.

STOCKINETTE STITCH AND REVERSE STOCKINETTE STITCH

Stockinette stitch is the pattern you see most often used for sweaters. It looks like rows of flat V's on the front, called the *right side*, and rows of bumps on the back, called the *wrong side*. Reverse stockinette stitch is the same as regular stockinette, only the bumpy side is considered the right side, and the smooth side is the wrong side.

1. Row 1 (right side): Knit.
2. Row 2 (wrong side): Purl.
3. Repeat rows 1 and 2 for stockinette stitch.

Stockininette stitch

Reverse Stockinette stitch

GARTER STITCH STRIPE

This pattern is essentially made up of two rows of stockinette stitch and two rows of garter stitch. It can be worked on any number of stitches. You can also vary the number of rows of stockinette stitch and garter stitch to create your own stripe pattern.

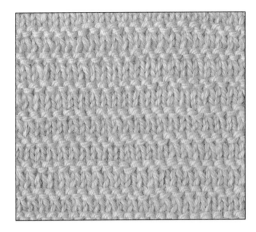

1 Row 1 (right side): Knit.

2 Row 2 (wrong side): Purl.

3 Row 3: Knit.

4 Row 4: Knit.

5 Repeat rows 1–4 for garter stitch stripe.

REVERSE STOCKINETTE STITCH STRIPE

This pattern looks similar to garter stitch stripe, but because the bumpy stripes are done in reverse stockinette stitch, they are fuller and rounder. You can work this pattern on any number of stitches.

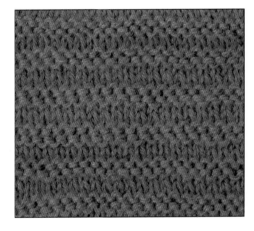

1 Row 1 (right side): Knit.

2 Row 2 (wrong side): Purl.

3 Row 3: Knit.

4 Row 4: Purl.

5 Row 5: Purl.

6 Row 6: Knit.

7 Repeat rows 1–6 for reverse stockinette stitch stripe.

CONTINUED ON NEXT PAGE

SEED STITCH

Seed stitch creates a nice bumpy-textured fabric that lies flat and looks the same on both sides. You knit the purl stitches and purl the knit stitches for seed stitch. You should cast on an even number of stitches.

1. Row 1 (right side): *Knit 1, purl 1; repeat from * to end of row.
2. Row 2 (wrong side): *Purl 1, knit 1; repeat from * to end of row.
3. Repeat rows 1 and 2 for seed stitch.

DOUBLE SEED STITCH

Double seed stitch is a four-row pattern that is similar to seed stitch in appearance but with larger texture. You work it on an even number of stitches.

1. Row 1 (right side): *Knit 1, purl 1; repeat from * to end of row.
2. Row 2 (wrong side): Repeat row 1.
3. Row 3: *Purl 1, knit 1; repeat from * to end of row.
4. Row 4: Repeat row 3.
5. Repeat rows 1–4 for double seed stitch.

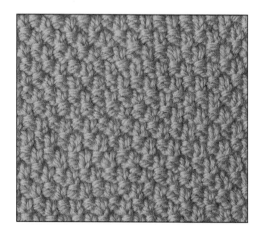

SIMPLE SEED STITCH

Simple seed stitch is a good allover pattern for sweaters, vests, and dresses. You work it over a multiple of 4 stitches plus 1 (that is, 9, 13, 17, and so on).

1 Row 1 (right side): Purl 1, *knit 3, purl 1; repeat from * to end.

2 Row 2 (wrong side): Purl.

3 Row 3: Knit.

4 Row 4: Purl.

5 Row 5: Knit 2, purl 1, *knit 3, purl 1; repeat from * to last 2 stitches, knit 2.

6 Row 6: Purl.

7 Row 7: Knit.

8 Row 8: Purl.

9 Repeat rows 1–8 for simple seed stitch.

BOX STITCH

Box stitch looks the same on both sides and lies flat. You work this pattern on a multiple of 4 stitches plus 2 (that is, 6, 10, 14, and so on).

1 Row 1 (right side): Knit 2, *purl 2, knit 2; repeat from * to end of row.

2 Row 2 (wrong side): Purl 2, *knit 2, purl 2; repeat from * to end of row.

3 Row 3: Repeat row 2.

4 Row 4: Repeat row 1.

5 Repeat rows 1–4 for box stitch.

Ribbing is used primarily for cuffs and hems because it is very elastic and won't stretch out or lose its shape. But ribbing patterns don't have to exclusively serve this purpose. They work very well as allover patterns on hats, pullovers, scarves, and blankets. You should try to get familiar with which stitches should be knit and which stitches should be purled.

Rib Patterns

1 X 1 RIB

For this 1 x 1 rib, you need to cast on an odd number of stitches. To keep the pattern correct, be sure to knit the stitches that look like V's and purl the stitches that look like bumps. This rib is commonly used on jacket cuffs, and it also works well for scarves.

1. Row 1 (right side): Knit 1, *purl 1, knit 1; repeat from * to end of row.
2. Row 2 (wrong side): Purl 1, *knit 1, purl 1; repeat from * to end of row.
3. Repeat rows 1 and 2 to create 1 x 1 rib.

2 X 2 RIB

You need a multiple of 4 stitches plus 2 (that is, 10, 14, 18, and so on) for this rib.

1. Row 1 (right side): Knit 2, *purl 2, knit 2; repeat from * to end of row.
2. Row 2 (wrong side): Purl 2, *knit 2, purl 2; repeat from * to end of row.
3. Repeat rows 1 and 2 to form 2 x 2 rib.

BROKEN RIB STITCH

This is an easy two-row pattern that looks very different on the front and on the back but is attractive on both sides. You work it on an odd number of stitches.

1 Row 1 (right side): Knit.

2 Row 2 (wrong side): Purl 1, *knit 1, purl 1; repeat from * to end of row.

3 Repeat rows 1 and 2 for broken rib stitch.

RIB-AND-RIDGE STITCH

This rib is not elastic, so it works best as an allover design. The right side looks like a rippled 1 x 1 rib, and the wrong side looks like an interrupted rib. You work this stitch pattern on a multiple of 2 stitches plus 1 (that is, 5, 7, 9, and so on).

1 Row 1 (wrong side): Purl.

2 Row 2 (right side): Knit.

3 Row 3: Knit 1, *purl 1, knit 1; repeat from * to end of row.

4 Row 4: Purl 1, *knit 1, purl 1; repeat from * to end of row.

5 Repeat rows 1–4 for rib-and-ridge stitch.

GARTER RIB

This stitch pattern does not look like most ribbing. It's very easy to do, and it looks the same on both sides. You work it on a multiple of 4 stitches plus 2 (that is, 6, 10, 14, and so on).

1 Row 1: Knit 2, *purl 2, knit 2; repeat from * to end.

2 Repeat row 1 for garter rib.

CONTINUED ON NEXT PAGE

SEEDED RIB

Seeded rib pattern is very attractive, and it results in a highly textured fabric. You work it over a multiple of 4 stitches plus 1 (that is, 9, 13, 17, and so on).

1. Row 1 (right side): Purl 1, *knit 3, purl 1; repeat from * to end.

2. Row 2 (wrong side): Knit 2, purl 1, *knit 3, purl 1; repeat from * to last 2 stitches, knit 2.

3. Repeat rows 1 and 2 for seeded rib.

TWISTED RIB

For twisted rib, you knit stitches through the back loops on right-side rows. You work it over an odd number of stitches.

1. Row 1 (right side): Knit 1 through back of loop, *purl 1, knit 1 through back of loop; repeat from * to end.

2. Row 2 (wrong side): Purl 1, *knit 1, purl 1; repeat from * to end.

3. Repeat rows 1 and 2 for twisted rib.

TWIN RIB

Twin rib pattern looks the same on both sides, even though the two rows that make up the pattern are different. It is good for just about anything—from jackets, sweaters, and dresses to scarves and bags. You work it on a multiple of 6 stitches.

1 Row 1 (right side): *Knit 3, purl 3; repeat from * to end.

2 Row 2 (wrong side): *Knit 1, purl 1; repeat from * to end.

3 Repeat rows 1 and 2 for twin rib.

DIAGONAL RIB

Diagonal rib is a pattern that can be used not only as a decorative border but also as an allover pattern. You work it over a multiple of 4 stitches.

1 Row 1 (right side): *Knit 2, purl 2; repeat from * to end.

2 Row 2 (wrong side): Repeat row 1.

3 Row 3: Knit 1, *purl 2, knit 2; repeat from * to last 3 stitches, purl 2, knit 1.

4 Row 4: Purl 1, *knit 2, purl 2; repeat from * to last 3 stitches, knit 2, purl 1.

5 Row 5: *Purl 2, knit 2; repeat from * to end.

6 Row 6: Repeat row 5.

7 Row 7: Repeat row 4.

8 Row 8: Repeat row 3.

9 Repeat rows 1–8 for diagonal rib.

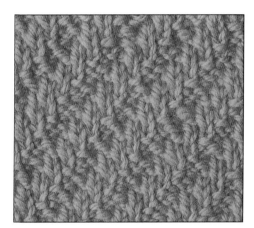

Try More Complicated Knit and Purl Stitch Patterns

You have already worked with some simple knit and purl combinations. Are you ready to try your hand at a few more? You can create some very intricate-looking patterns by following these simple instructions.

More Complicated Knit and Purl Stitch Patterns

ANDALUSIAN STITCH

This stitch creates a nice grid pattern and is easy to do. You work it on a multiple of 2 stitches plus 1 (that is, 5, 7, 9, and so on).

1. Row 1 (right side): Knit.
2. Row 2 (wrong side): Purl.
3. Row 3: *Knit 1, purl 1; repeat from * to last stitch, knit 1.
4. Row 4: Purl.
5. Repeat rows 1–4 for Andalusian stitch.

RICE STITCH

This is an easy allover pattern that lies flat and looks like ribbing on the wrong side. You work it over a multiple of 2 stitches plus 1 (that is, 5, 7, 9, and so on).

1. Row 1 (right side): Purl 1, *knit 1 through back of loop, purl 1; repeat from * to end.
2. Row 2 (wrong side): Knit.
3. Repeat rows 1 and 2 for rice stitch.

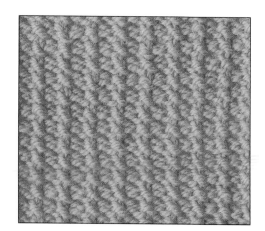

SMALL BASKETWEAVE

There are many forms of basketweave. This one is a small weave that you work on a multiple of 4 stitches plus 3 (that is, 11, 15, 19, and so on).

1️⃣ Row 1 (right side): Knit.

2️⃣ Row 2 (wrong side): *Knit 3, purl 1; repeat from * to last 3 stitches, knit 3.

3️⃣ Row 3: Knit.

4️⃣ Row 4: Knit 1, *purl 1, knit 3; repeat from * to last 2 stitches, purl 1, knit 1.

5️⃣ Repeat rows 1–4 for small basketweave.

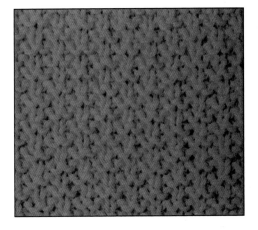

CHECKERBOARD PATTERN

This pattern looks the same on both sides. You work this particular checkerboard on a multiple of 8 stitches plus 4 (that is, 20, 28, 36, and so on).

1️⃣ Row 1 (right side): Knit 4, *purl 4, knit 4; repeat from * to end.

2️⃣ Row 2 (wrong side): Purl 4, *knit 4, purl 4; repeat from * to end.

3️⃣ Row 3: Repeat row 1.

4️⃣ Row 4: Repeat row 2.

5️⃣ Row 5: Repeat row 2.

6️⃣ Row 6: Repeat row 1.

7️⃣ Row 7: Repeat row 2.

8️⃣ Row 8: Repeat row 1.

9️⃣ Repeat rows 1–8 for checkerboard pattern.

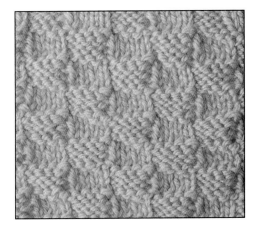

DIAGONAL CHECK PATTERN

This pattern, worked over a multiple of 5 stitches, looks the same on both sides.

1️⃣ Row 1 (right side): *Purl 1, knit 4; repeat from * to end.

2️⃣ Row 2 (wrong side): *Purl 3, knit 2; repeat from * to end.

3️⃣ Row 3: Repeat row 2.

4️⃣ Row 4: Repeat row 1.

5️⃣ Row 5: *Knit 1, purl 4; repeat from * to end.

6️⃣ Row 6: *Knit 3, purl 2; repeat from * to end.

7️⃣ Row 7: Repeat row 6.

8️⃣ Row 8: Repeat row 5.

9️⃣ Repeat rows 1–8 for diagonal check pattern.

CONTINUED ON NEXT PAGE

DIAMOND BROCADE PATTERN

This is a very elegant allover pattern. You work it on a multiple of 8 stitches plus 1 (that is, 17, 25, 33, and so on).

1. Row 1 (right side): Knit 4, *purl 1, knit 7; repeat from * to last 5 stitches, purl 1, knit 4.

2. Row 2 (wrong side): Purl 3, *knit 1, purl 1, knit 1, purl 5; repeat from * to last 6 stitches, knit 1, purl 1, knit 1, purl 3.

3. Row 3: Knit 2, *purl 1, knit 3; repeat from * to last 3 stitches, purl 1, knit 2.

4. Row 4: Purl 1, *knit 1, purl 5, knit 1, purl 1; repeat from * to end.

5. Row 5: *Purl 1, knit 7; repeat from * to last stitch, purl 1.

6. Row 6: Repeat row 4.

7. Row 7: Repeat row 3.

8. Row 8: Repeat row 2.

9. Repeat rows 1–8 for diamond brocade pattern.

DIAMONDS IN COLUMNS

You can repeat any motif in a series of panels. This one works well on sweaters, vests, and pillows. You work this pattern on a multiple of 8 stitches plus 1 (that is, 17, 25, 33, and so on).

1. Row 1 (right side): Knit.

2. Row 2 (wrong side): Knit 1, *purl 7, knit 1; repeat from * to end.

3. Row 3: Knit 4, *purl 1, knit 7; repeat from * to last 5 stitches, purl 1, knit 4.

4. Row 4: Knit 1, *purl 2, knit 1, purl 1, knit 1, purl 2, knit 1; repeat from * to end.

5. Row 5: Knit 2, *[purl 1, knit 1] twice, purl 1, knit 3; repeat from * to last 7 stitches, [purl 1, knit 1] twice, purl 1, knit 2.

6. Row 6: Repeat row 4.

7. Row 7: Repeat row 3.

8. Row 8: Repeat row 2.

9. Repeat rows 1–8 for diamonds in columns pattern.

LINEN STITCH

This is a marvelous stitch pattern that has a woven look on one side and a grid of bumps on the other. It lies flat and is wonderful for sweaters, blankets, bags, and scarves. You work it over an even number of stitches.

1. Row 1 (right side): *Knit 1, slip 1 purlwise with yarn at front of work, bring yarn to back of work between needles; repeat from * to last 2 stitches, knit 2.

2. Row 2 (wrong side): *Purl 1, slip 1 purlwise with yarn at back of work, bring yarn to front of work between needles; repeat from * to last 2 stitches, purl 2.

3. Repeat rows 1 and 2 for linen stitch.

VERTICAL DASH STITCH

Vertical dash stitch works well as an allover pattern for sweaters, skirts, and dresses. You work it on a multiple of 6 stitches plus 1 (that is, 13, 19, 25, and so on).

1. Row 1 (right side): Purl 3, knit 1, *purl 5, knit 1; repeat from * to last 3 stitches, purl 3.

2. Row 2 (wrong side): Knit 3, purl 1, *knit 5, purl 1; repeat from * to last 3 stitches, knit 3.

3. Row 3: Repeat row 1.

4. Row 4: Repeat row 2.

5. Row 5: Knit 1, *purl 5, knit 1; repeat from * to end.

6. Row 6: Purl 1, *knit 5, purl 1; repeat from * to end.

7. Row 7: Repeat row 5.

8. Row 8: Repeat row 6.

9. Repeat rows 1–8 for vertical dash stitch.

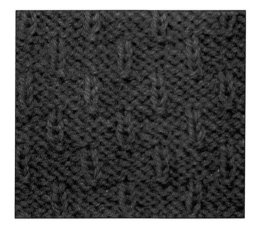

SINGLE CHEVRON STITCH

Single chevron stitch is a nice, playful pattern that works well on pullovers, cardigans, and vests. You work it over a multiple of 8 stitches.

1. Row 1 (right side): *Purl 1, knit 3; repeat from * to end.

2. Row 2 (wrong side): *Knit 1, purl 5, knit 1, purl 1; repeat from * to end.

3. Row 3: *Knit 2, purl 1, knit 3, purl 1, knit 1; repeat from * to end.

4. Row 4: *Purl 2, knit 1, purl 1, knit 1, purl 3; repeat from * to end.

5. Repeat rows 1–4 for single chevron stitch.

chapter 4

Shaping

Now that you have learned some basic techniques, such as combining knitting and purling to create interesting patterns, you're ready to learn about increasing and decreasing to shape your knitting beyond just a rectangle. It's not hard, and once you master a few increase and decrease methods, you'll be able to make a sweater. Take some time to experiment.

Increase 1 Stitch

To make your knitting wider, you need to *increase*, or add, a stitch or stitches. There are many types of increases, each with a different appearance or purpose.

You can keep track of when to increase more easily when you do it on the same side (usually the front side) every time, and you can better see how it will look finished. It is also a good idea to perform increases a couple stitches in from the beginning or end of a row, so as not to create an uneven edge.

Bar Increase

This increase is called a *bar increase* because it creates a visible horizontal bar of yarn where the increase is made. You should knit 1 or 2 stitches at the beginning of the row before making a bar increase.

① Insert the right needle into the next stitch and knit it, except don't bring the old stitch up and off the left needle (a); then insert the right needle into the back of the same stitch and knit it again (b).

② Bring the stitch you knit into twice off the left needle.

You should have 2 new stitches on the right needle: the one you knit into the front of the stitch and the one you knit into the back of it.

Yarn Over

Yarn over is an increase that is often used for decorative increases and lacy patterns because it makes a hole.

YARN OVER WITH KNIT STITCH

1. To do a yarn over before a knit stitch, bring the working yarn to the front of the needles and lay it over the right needle from front to back.

2. Knit the next stitch.

   Laying the yarn over the right needle creates another stitch. On the next row, just knit it or purl it as usual.

YARN OVER WITH PURL STITCH

1. To do a yarn over before a purl stitch, bring the working yarn to the front of the needles, wrap it over and under the right needle, and bring it back to the front to be ready to purl.

2. Purl the next stitch.

   Laying the yarn over the right needle creates another stitch. On the next row, just knit it or purl it as usual.

FINISHED INCREASE

After you work a couple rows, you see the hole that the yarn over created.

CONTINUED ON NEXT PAGE

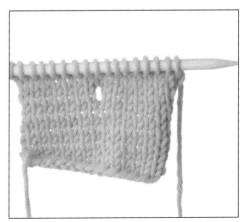

Make One: Right Slanting

You can make some increases that are barely visible. One such increase, the make one, involves lifting the horizontal strand between 2 stitches up onto the left needle and knitting it. This version slants to the right.

RIGHT-SLANTING MAKE ONE WITH KNIT STITCH

1. Before a knit stitch, use the left needle to pick up the horizontal strand *from back to front* between the last stitch worked on the right needle and the next stitch to be worked on the left needle.

2. Insert the right needle into the front of the strand and knit it.

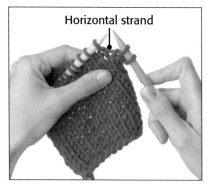
Horizontal strand

RIGHT-SLANTING MAKE ONE WITH PURL STITCH

1. Before a purl stitch, use the left needle to pick up the horizontal strand *from back to front* between the last stitch worked on the right needle and the next stitch to be worked on the left needle.

2. Insert the right needle into the front of the strand and purl it.

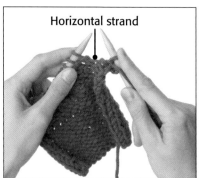
Horizontal strand

FINISHED INCREASE

After you work a few rows, you can see how this increase slants to the right.

Right-slanting make one

Make One: Left Slanting

A left-slanting make one is just like a right-slanting make one, except the horizontal strand is picked up from front to back.

LEFT-SLANTING MAKE ONE WITH KNIT STITCH

1. Before a knit stitch, use the left needle to pick up the horizontal strand *from front to back* between the last stitch worked on the right needle and the next stitch to be worked from the left needle.

2. Insert the right needle into the back of the loop and knit it.

RIGHT-SLANTING MAKE ONE WITH PURL STITCH

1. Before a purl stitch, pick up the horizontal strand with the left needle, *from front to back*.

2. Insert the right needle into the back of the loop *from back to front* and purl it.

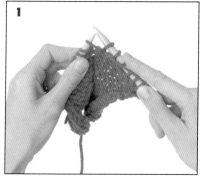

FINISHED INCREASE

After you work a few rows, you can see how this increase slants to the left.

Left-slanting make one

Increase Multiple Stitches

Sometimes you need to increase more than 1 or 2 stitches across a row, or you need to increase 2 stitches at a time to shape your knitting in a symmetrical way.

How to Increase Multiple Stitches

DOUBLE BAR INCREASE

This increase is called a double bar increase because you use the bar increase method twice in one row to shape symmetrically. It is usually done over an odd number of stitches, on the front side of a piece of knitting, and in the center of the row of knitting. For a refresher on bar increases, see page 48.

1 Knit across to the stitch *before* the center stitch (known as the *axis stitch*) and then work a bar increase.

2 Work a second bar increase into the center stitch. Knit to the end of the row.

Even though the second increase is worked on the axis stitch, the bar appears after it.

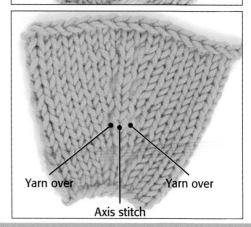

DOUBLE MAKE ONE INCREASE

This increase is similar to the double bar increase in that you increase 1 stitch on either side of an axis stitch, but it is less visible. It is also worked on the front side of a piece of knitting, over an odd number of stitches. For a refresher on make one increases, see pages 50–51.

1 Knit across to the axis stitch. Perform a right-slanting make one increase, using the horizontal strand between the last stitch worked and the axis stitch.

2 Knit the axis stitch.

3 Perform a left-slanting make one increase, using the horizontal strand between the axis stitch and the next stitch to be worked on the left needle. Knit to the end of the row.

DOUBLE YARN OVER INCREASE

The double yarn over increase is similar to the two previous double increases in that you work increases on either side of an axis stitch. For a refresher on basic yarn over stitches, see page 49.

1 Knit across to the axis stitch. Perform a yarn over.

2 Knit the axis stitch.

3 Perform another yarn over. Knit to the end of the row.

INCREASING MULTIPLE STITCHES EVENLY ACROSS A ROW

Some patterns ask you to increase a certain number of stitches evenly across a row. This is called for when the knitting needs to become substantially wider quickly, rather than gradually. You should use whichever increase method is best suited to your stitch pattern.

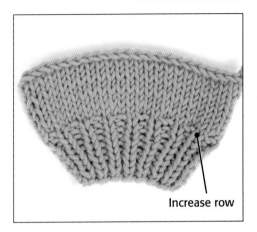

1 To figure out how to increase a certain number of stitches evenly across a row, start by adding 1 to the number of stitches that need to be added.

2 Divide the number obtained in step 1 into the number of stitches on your needles. The result of this division is how many stitches you should work between increases across the row. (For example, if you have 30 stitches on your needle and you are asked to increase 5 stitches evenly across, then you knit 5 stitches, increase 1, knit 5, and so on.)

3 If the result of your equation is not exact, you need to approximate and work fewer stitches between some of the increases. The most important thing is to spread the correct number of increases across the row as evenly as possible.

Increase row

 FAQ

What if I need to increase more than 2 stitches at the beginning or the end of a row?

Some garments require increasing multiple stitches at one or both ends of a piece of knitting. In that case, you cannot use the increase methods covered here. Instead, you have to cast on the number of increases called for, using the simple cast-on method (see page 15).

1. Before knitting the row, cast on the number of stitches required in front of the stitches already on the needle.

2. Knit the newly cast-on stitches as usual.

Note: If the instructions call for increasing stitches at both ends of the row, you cast on that number of stitches at the beginning of the next two rows because you can't cast on at the end of a row.

Decrease 1 Stitch

When you need to make your knitting narrower, you *decrease* stitches. There are several methods for decreasing, each with different effects. You should take some time to practice the different methods so you can see how they transform your knitting.

Knit 2 Together/Purl 2 Together

These are two of the most commonly used decreases. The knit 2 together is performed with knit stitches, and the purl 2 together is performed with purl stitches. Both decreases can be used at any point in a row of knitting or purling. This decrease, either knit or purled, slants somewhat to the right on the front side of a piece of knitting.

KNIT 2 TOGETHER

① Insert the right needle into the front of the next 2 stitches (as if to knit) on the left needle.

② Wrap the yarn around the right needle and knit the 2 stitches as 1 stitch.

PURL 2 TOGETHER

① Insert the right needle from back to front into the front of the next 2 stitches (as if to purl) on the left needle.

② Wrap the yarn around the right needle and purl the 2 stitches as 1 stitch.

Knit or Purl 2 Together Through Back of Loop

These two decreases are similar to the regular knit 2 together and purl 2 together decreases, only in this case, the 2 stitches are worked together through the back of the loops instead of through the front. They both result in a left-slanting decrease on the front side of a piece of knitting.

KNIT 2 TOGETHER THROUGH BACK OF LOOP

1 Insert the right needle from front to back into the back of the next 2 stitches on the left needle.

2 Knit the 2 stitches together as 1 stitch.

PURL 2 TOGETHER THROUGH BACK OF LOOP

1 Insert the right needle from back to front into the back of the next 2 stitches on the left needle.

2 Purl the 2 stitches together as 1 stitch.

FINISHED DECREASE

A knit 2 together or a purl 2 together decrease results in shaping that slants to the right (a) on the front side of a piece of knitting. A knit 2 together through back of loop or a purl 2 together through back of loop decrease results in shaping that slants to the left (b) on the front side of a piece of knitting.

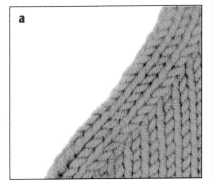

a
b

CONTINUED ON NEXT PAGE

Slip, Slip, Knit

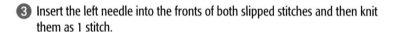

This decrease is practically invisible. It is worked on the front side of a piece of knitting, and it slants to the left. If you want to shape your knitting on both sides symmetrically, you can begin the row with a slip, slip, knit and end the row with a knit 2 together.

① Insert the right needle from front to back into the front of the next stitch on the left needle and slip it onto the right needle.

② Repeat step 1.

You have slipped 2 stitches from the left needle to the right needle.

③ Insert the left needle into the fronts of both slipped stitches and then knit them as 1 stitch.

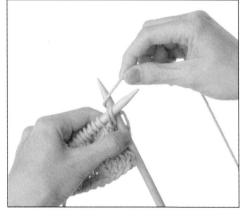

You can see that the slip, slip, knit decrease slants subtly to the left.

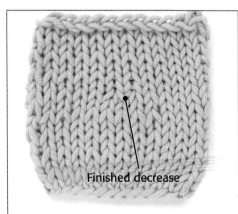

Finished decrease

Slip 1, Knit 1, Pass Slipped Stitch Over

This decrease, also worked on the front side of a piece of knitting, slants quite visibly to the left. It is also sometimes referred to as slip, knit, pass.

1 Insert the right needle from front to back into the front of the next stitch on the left needle and slip it onto the right needle.

2 Knit the next stitch from the left needle.

3 Insert the left needle into the front of the slipped stitch and bring the slipped stitch over the knit stitch and off the needle.

You can see that the slip 1, knit 1, pass slipped stitch over decrease slants markedly to the left.

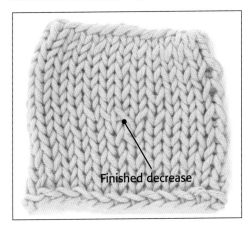

Finished decrease

Decrease Multiple Stitches

You may want to decrease more than 1 stitch at a time over one row. Your instructions may call for decreasing many stitches across a row, which results in a gathered look; or you may need to decrease 2 stitches in tandem over a series of rows, for more gradual shaping.

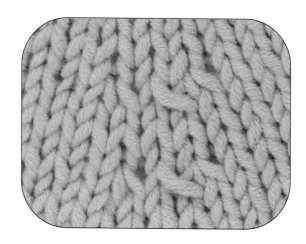

How to Decrease Multiple Stitches

DECREASING MULTIPLE STITCHES ACROSS ONE ROW

Some instructions may direct you to decrease a certain number of stitches evenly across a row.

1 To figure out how to decrease a certain number of stitches evenly across a row, divide the number of stitches you have on your needles by the number you need to decrease.

2 Subtract 2 from the result, and that is the number of stitches you need to work between decreases. (For example, if you have 30 stitches on your needles and you are asked to decrease 10 stitches evenly across, then you will knit 1 stitch, work the decrease over the next 2 stitches, knit 1 stitch, and so on.)

This example illustrates what decreasing the number of stitches by half looks like.

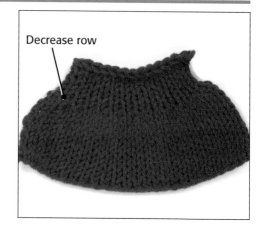

Decrease row

BASIC DOUBLE DECREASE

Remember when you increased 2 stitches at once, on either side of an axis stitch? You can also decrease 2 stitches at once by using an axis stitch. You work this double decrease on the right side.

1 Work a slip, slip, knit decrease over the 2 stitches before the axis stitch.

2 Knit the axis stitch.

3 Knit together the next 2 stitches after the axis stitch.

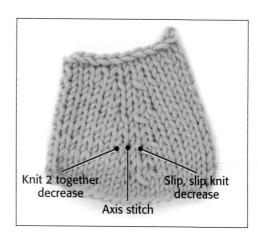

Knit 2 together decrease

Axis stitch

Slip, slip knit decrease

DOUBLE VERTICAL DECREASE

This double decrease results in symmetrical shaping with a raised vertical stitch in the center. It is worked on the right side. It is sometimes called slip 2, knit 1, pass 2 slipped stitches over.

1 Insert the right needle into the next 2 stitches on the left needle as if to knit them together and then slip them off the left needle and onto the right needle.

2 Knit the next stitch from the left needle.

3 Use the left needle to pick up both slipped stitches at the same time and pass them over the knit stitch and off the right needle.

You can see here how the double vertical decrease looks when performed over a progression of rows. The purl rows are worked without decreasing.

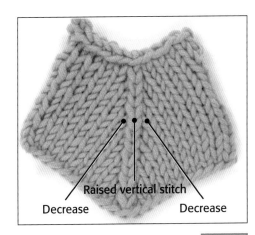

Raised vertical stitch

Decrease   Decrease

Shape with Short-Rowing

Short-rowing is a shaping technique that involves working a series of partial rows—instead of decreasing or increasing stitches—to create curved or slanted edges. Short-rowing eliminates the jagged stair steps that occur when binding off a series of stitches over a few rows, so it's an excellent choice for shaped shoulders and necklines. Short-rowing is also commonly used to shape baby booties, sock heels, and bonnets.

How to Shape with Short-Rowing: Knit Side

1 Work across the row to the point where the work should be turned. Keeping the working yarn at the back of the work, slip the next stitch from the left needle—as you would to purl—to the right needle.

2 Bring the working yarn between the needles to the front of the work.

3 Slip the same stitch you slipped in step 1 back to the left needle.

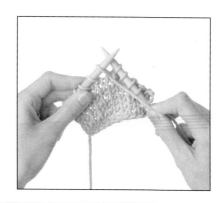

④ Bring the working yarn to the back of the work, thereby wrapping the slipped stitch.

⑤ Turn your work so that you're ready to work the wrong side.

CONTINUED ON NEXT PAGE

TIP

Preventing Holes When Short-Rowing

Short-rowing involves working partway across a row, turning the work to the other side, working back partway, and repeating this until you have achieved the desired shaping. To prevent holes from appearing at the turning points, you slip and wrap the turning stitches as shown here.

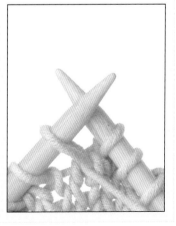

How to Shape with Short-Rowing: Purl Side

1 Work across the row to the point where the work should be turned. Keeping the working yarn at the front of the work, slip the next stitch from the left needle—as you would to purl—to the right needle.

2 Bring the working yarn between the needles to the back of the work.

3 Slip the same stitch you slipped in step 1 back to the left needle.

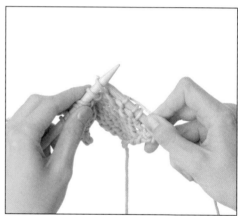

4 Bring the working yarn to the front of the work, thereby wrapping the slipped stitch.

How to Hide Short-Row Wraps

After you complete a short row, you need to hide your wraps so that your work looks tidy.

HIDING SHORT-ROW WRAPS ON THE KNIT SIDE

1 On the knit side, work to the point where the wrap is.

2 Insert the right needle knitwise under both the wrap and the wrapped stitch.

3 Knit the wrap and the wrapped stitch as 1 stitch.

HIDING SHORT-ROW WRAPS ON THE PURL SIDE

1 On the purl side, work to the point where the wrap is.

2 Insert the right needle from back to front through the back loop of the wrap. Lift the wrap and place it onto the left needle with the wrapped stitch.

3 Purl the wrap and the wrapped stitch as 1 stitch.

After you complete your short-row shaping, you can bind off or continue your pattern as established.

Note: *Shoulders that have been shaped with short rows can be grafted together for a more seamless look (see page 142).*

chapter 5

Correcting Mistakes

Has a mysterious hole appeared in your knitting? Or do you have fewer stitches on your needle than you should? Dropped stitches, twisted stitches, incomplete stitches—these are all common errors beginners (and even experts!) make. You can fix them easily, using the following methods.

Correct Twisted Stitches

Sometimes stitches become twisted, resulting in an uneven finish to the knit fabric. To recognize the problem, you need to familiarize yourself with how stitches should sit on the needle. When you look at the stitches on your needle, the right side of each loop should rest on the front of the needle, and the left side of each loop should rest against the back of the needle. If you see a stitch where the left side of the loop is in front, you have a twisted stitch.

How to Correct Twisted Stitches

① Work across the stitches from the left needle until you get to the twisted stitch.

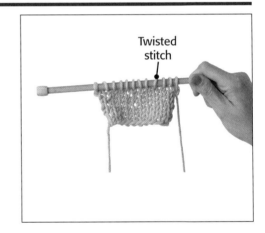

Twisted stitch

② Use the right needle to pick up the twisted stitch from the left needle (a), turn it around, and place it back on the left needle so that the right side of the loop is in front (b).

a

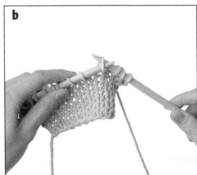

b

Correct Incomplete Stitches

A stitch is *incomplete* when the working yarn does not get pulled through the loop. The stitch gets transferred but is not knit or purled, and the working yarn is wrapped over the needle, crossing over the mistakenly slipped stitch.

How to Correct Incomplete Stitches

1 Work across the stitches from the left needle until you get to the incomplete stitch.

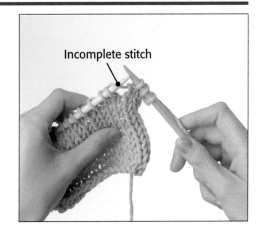

Incomplete stitch

2 Insert the right needle as if to purl (from back to front) into the incomplete stitch (a). Pull it over the unworked strand (b) and off the needle.

a

b

Pick Up Dropped Stitches

You have probably dropped a stitch or two by now. A *dropped stitch* is a stitch that has slipped off your needles. Dropped stitches can unravel down vertically through many rows, so it's important to learn how to fix them.

When you realize that you have dropped a stitch on the row before the row you're currently working, you can fix it with your knitting needle. If you dropped a stitch more than one row ago, causing a *run*, you need a crochet hook to fix it.

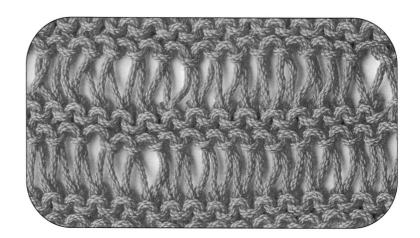

How to Pick Up a Dropped Stitch One Row Below

① Work across the stitches from the left needle until you get to the dropped stitch.

② Insert the right needle into the dropped stitch and under the horizontal strand (the "ladder") behind the dropped stitch.

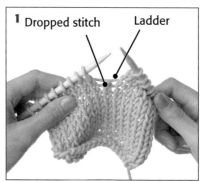

1 Dropped stitch   Ladder

2

③ Insert the left needle from back to front into the dropped stitch on the right needle and pull it over the ladder and off the right needle.

④ Use the right needle to transfer the repaired stitch back to the left needle.

The repaired stitch is ready to be worked as usual.

3

4

How to Pick Up a Dropped Purl Stitch One Row Below

1️⃣ Work across the stitches on the left needle until you get to the dropped stitch.

2️⃣ Insert the right needle into the dropped stitch, as if to purl, and under the horizontal strand (the "ladder") in front of the dropped stitch.

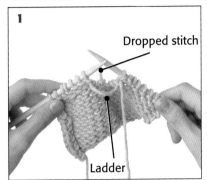

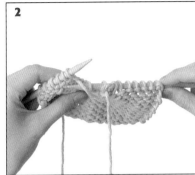

Dropped stitch

Ladder

3️⃣ Use the left needle to lift the dropped stitch on the right needle up over the ladder and off the right needle.

4️⃣ Insert the left needle into the back of the repaired stitch to transfer it back to the left needle.

The repaired stitch is ready to be worked as usual.

CONTINUED ON NEXT PAGE

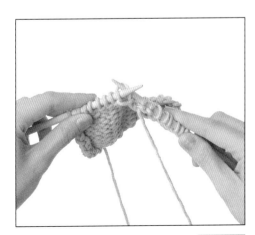

How to Pick Up a Dropped Stitch Several Rows Below

A dropped stitch that has unraveled several or more rows is called a *run*. To repair a run, you can use a crochet hook that is the appropriate size for the yarn you're using. If you're working on the purl side when you discover the run, you just turn your work to the knit side to correct it.

1 Work across the stitches from the left needle until you get to where the dropped stitch should be.

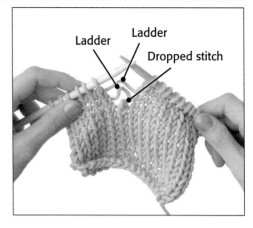

Ladder   Ladder   Dropped stitch

2 Insert the crochet hook from front to back into the dropped stitch. Pull the lowest horizontal ladder from back to front through the dropped stitch.

3 Repeat step 2 until you have no more ladders left.

4 Place the repaired stitch onto the left needle, being sure not to twist it.

The repaired stitch is ready to be worked as usual.

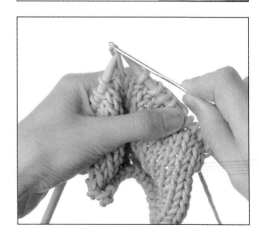

How to Pick Up a Dropped Edge Stitch Several Rows Below

An edge stitch that has been dropped and let run for several rows has a different appearance from a run down the interior of a piece of knitting. Instead of seeing a row of horizontal ladders, you see two loops at the edge: the dropped stitch and a large loop of yarn at the edge. For this repair, too, you use a crochet hook that is the appropriate size for the yarn you're using.

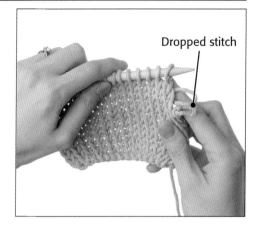

Dropped stitch

① Insert the crochet hook from front to back through the dropped stitch. Pull the big loop through it to the front.

② Repeat step 1 until you get to the top.

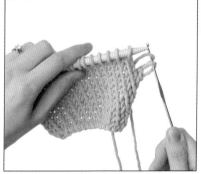

③ Use the crochet hook to pull the working yarn through the last stitch created.

④ Use the crochet hook to place the repaired stitch back onto the left needle.

The repaired stitch is ready to be worked as usual.

Unravel Stitches

If you make an error that can't be fixed by using any of the previous methods, you probably need to unravel some of your work. For example, if you are working a particular stitch pattern and make a mistake in your pattern that is visibly wrong, you can unravel back to that point and correct it. If you make an error that is on the same row that you're working on, you can unravel stitch by stitch.

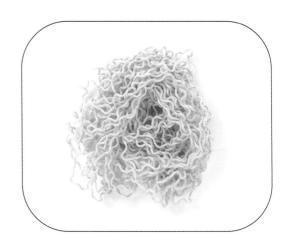

How to Unravel Stitch by Stitch

When you get good at unraveling stitch by stitch, it will feel like you're knitting backward, or "un-knitting."

UNRAVELING STITCH BY STITCH ON THE KNIT SIDE

1 On the knit side, hold the working yarn in back and insert the left needle from front to back into the stitch in the row below the next stitch on the right needle.

2 Drop the stitch above off the right needle and pull the working yarn to un-knit it.

UNRAVELING STITCH BY STITCH ON THE PURL SIDE

1 On the purl side, hold the working yarn in front and insert the left needle from front to back into the stitch in the row below the next stitch on the right needle.

2 Drop the stitch above off the right needle and pull the working yarn to un-purl it.

How to Unravel Row by Row

If you make an error that is more than one row down from where you are currently working, you need to unravel row by row.

1 Slide the stitches off the needle and pull the working yarn until you have unraveled the desired number of rows.

2 Using a needle that is smaller in diameter than the working needle, carefully slide the stitches back onto that needle. Take care not to twist the stitches when you put them back onto the needle.

You can now resume knitting with the working needles.

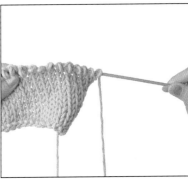

TIP

A Safer Way to Unravel

To avoid dropping stitches as you unravel, you can use another method: You can weave a needle that is smaller in diameter than the working needles in and out of the stitches in the row below the point to which you would like to unravel (a). You need to be sure the needle goes under the right side of each stitch and over the left side of each stitch. When the entire row is on the needle, you pull the working yarn to unravel the rows above the needle (b). You can then resume knitting with the working needles.

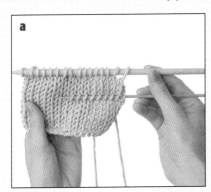

a

b

chapter 6

Learning to Read Written Instructions

By now you've probably looked at some knitting pattern books or leaflets and thought, "Is this in English?" Knitting instructions use a lot of terms and abbreviations that are unfamiliar and intimidating at first. This chapter will enable you to understand what you are reading the next time you look at a knitting pattern.

When you're ready to knit something where size and fit are crucial, you need to understand gauge. *Gauge* (referred to as *tension* in the UK) is the number of stitches and rows per inch—using stockinette stitch, unless the pattern notes otherwise. Different yarns knit to different gauges, the same yarn knits to a different gauge on different sizes of needles, and different knitters knit the same yarn on the same needles at different gauges.

Understanding Gauge

A good knitting pattern will specify the gauge required to attain the desired size or fit of the garment. For example, it will read something like "Gauge: 20 stitches and 30 rows to 4 inches over stockinette stitch on size 7 (4.5mm) needles." In order for you to create the sweater or hat so that it comes out in the same measurements that the pattern specifies and so that it fits properly, you need to be sure that you are knitting to that same gauge. Though your yarn label should indicate what size needle to use with the yarn and what the desired gauge is, you should use that recommendation only as a guide, as tension varies from knitter to knitter.

These three swatches were all made using 20 stitches and 30 rows, but with different yarns and different needle sizes. You can see how varied the sizes of the final results are. That's why making sure you're getting the same gauge the pattern calls for—with the yarn you have chosen for the project—is so important. Even a slight discrepancy can have a tremendous effect. A 1-stitch-per-inch difference in gauge, over a large number of stitches, can result in a final size that is several inches smaller or larger than desired.

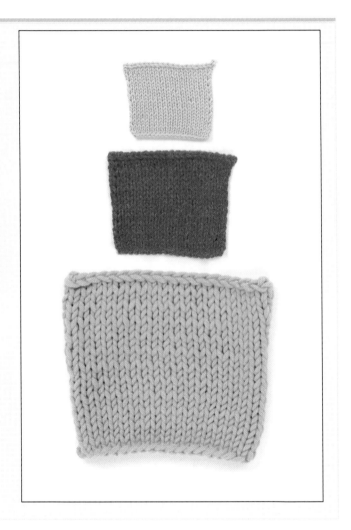

Understanding How Gauge Can Differ with Various Stitch Patterns

Sometimes a knitting pattern will cite the gauge for a particular stitch pattern, if that's what is primarily used for that garment. Like needle size and type of yarn, stitch pattern can also affect gauge. For example, the same yarn, worked in stockinette stitch on size 7 needles, knits to a different gauge in a ribbed pattern on the same size needles.

These three swatches are all made from the same yarn and using the same needles, over 20 stitches and 30 rows, but with different stitch patterns. You can see how varied the sizes of the final results are.

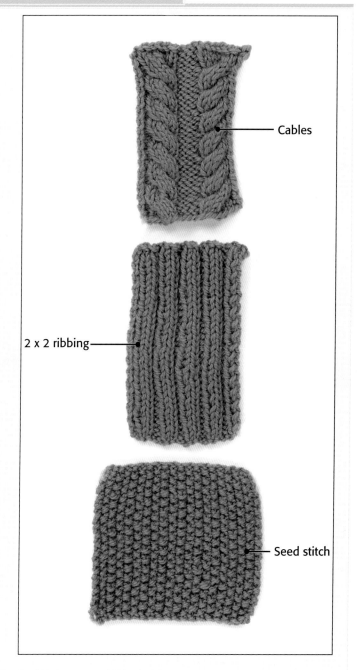

Cables

2 x 2 ribbing

Seed stitch

Make and Measure a Gauge Swatch

Before starting a project, you should always make a gauge swatch to ensure that you are knitting to the gauge the pattern calls for. A *gauge swatch* is a small square of knitting used to measure how many stitches and rows per inch you are getting with a particular yarn on a certain size needle. It takes only a few minutes to make one, and you will definitely not regret it. Many new knitters skip this step and spend hours on a sweater that ends up too big or too small.

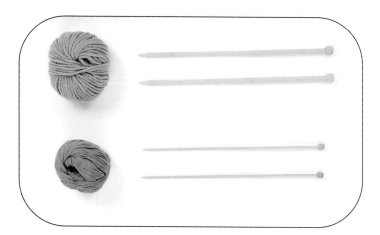

How to Make a Gauge Swatch

To make a gauge swatch, you need to use the yarn and needle size that the pattern calls for. It's not a bad idea to have handy three pairs of needles: the size called for, the next size smaller, and the next size larger. (If you don't use them for this project, you will need them someday for another project.)

1 Cast on the same number of stitches that the pattern says is equal to 4.

2 Work in stockinette stitch (knit on the right side and purl on the wrong side) until the swatch is 4 inches long (measuring from the cast-on edge to the needle).

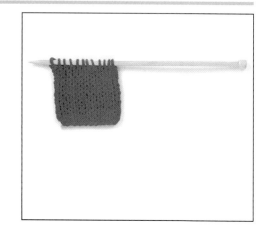

3 Bind off your stitches somewhat loosely, cut the working yarn (leaving about a 6-inch tail), and pull the tail through the last stitch.

How to Measure a Gauge Swatch

Remember the stitch and needle gauge tool from Chapter 1? Now is the time to use it. If you don't have one, you can use a ruler or tape measure. Also, if your gauge swatch is curly and won't lie flat, and if your yarn's care instructions allow, take a warm steam iron to the swatch, pressing only lightly. Let it cool and dry.

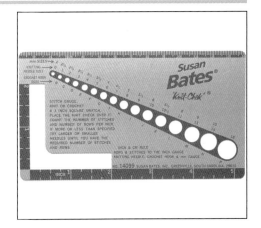

1 Lay your swatch on a flat surface. Place your stitch and needle gauge (or other measuring device) so that the opening is centered both horizontally and vertically on the swatch.

2 Count how many stitches there are in the horizontal 2-inch space and how many rows there are in the vertical 2-inch space.

3 Divide these numbers by 2, and that is the number of stitches and rows you are getting *per inch.*

4 If your pattern lists gauge as a certain number of stitches and rows over 4 inches, just multiply your stitch and row counts for 2 inches by 2.

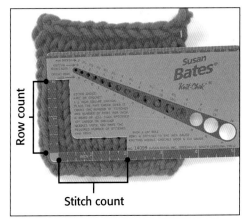

Row count

Stitch count

FAQ

What should I do if my gauge is different from the gauge listed in the pattern?

If you are getting more stitches per 4 inches than the pattern calls for, try switching to a needle that is one size larger. If you are getting fewer stitches per 4 inches than the pattern calls for, try switching to a needle that is one size smaller. Make a new gauge swatch

and measure again. If necessary, go up or down another needle size, create a new swatch, and remeasure.

It is difficult to match both stitch and row gauge, but it is more important to match the stitch gauge accurately. If the row gauge is slightly off, bear in mind that when you're working vertically, you may have to go more by the garment's measurements than by the row counts.

Knitting Abbreviations and Terms

The more you knit, the more familiar knitting language will become. You've probably looked at knitting instructions and wondered what all those abbreviations stand for. You can use this guide to become familiar with common terms and abbreviations.

KNITTING ABBREVIATIONS

Abbreviation	Meaning	Abbreviation	Meaning
alt	alternate	foll	follow(s); following
approx	approximately	g; gr	gram(s)
BC	back cross	grp	group
beg	beginning	g st	garter stitch
bet	between	hdc	half double crochet
BO	bind off	htr	half treble (crochet)
C	cable; cross; contrast color	in(s)	inch(es)
cab	cable	inc(s)	increase(s); increasing
CB	cable back	incl	including
CC	contrast color	k	knit
CF	cable front	k1b	knit into back of stitch
ch	chain; crochet hook	k2tog	knit 2 stitches together
circ	circular	k3tog	knit 3 stitches together
cm	centimeter(s)	kfb; kf&b	knit into front and back of stitch
cn	cable needle	k tbl	knit through back of loop
CO	cast on	kwise	knitwise
cont	continue(s); continuing	l	left
cr l	cross left	LC	left cross
cr r	cross right	LH	left-hand
dbl	double (crochet)	lp(s)	loop(s)
dc	double cross	LT	left twist
dec(s)	decrease(s); decreasing	M	main color
diag	diagonal	m1	make one
diam	diameter	mb	make bobble
DK	double knitting	MC	main color
dpn(s)	double-pointed needle(s)	med	medium
dtr	double treble (crochet)	mm	millimeter(s)
epi	ends per inch	mult	multiple
FC	front cross	no	number

Abbreviation	Meaning
opp	opposite
oz	ounce
p	purl
p1b	purl into back of stitch
p2sso	pass 2 slipped stitches over
p2tog	purl 2 stitches together
p3tog	purl 3 stitches together
pat; patt	pattern
pfb	purl into front and back of stitch
pm	place marker
prev	previous
psso	pass slipped stitch over
p tbl	purl through back of loop
pu	pick up
pwise	purlwise
RC	right cross
rem	remain; remaining
rep(s)	repeat(s)
rev	reverse
rev St st	reverse stockinette stitch
RH	right-hand
rib	ribbing
rnd(s)	round(s)
RS	right side
RT	right twist
sc	single crochet
sel; selv	selvage
sk	skip
skp; skpo	slip 1, knit 1, pass slipped stitch over
sl	slip

Abbreviation	Meaning
sl st	slip(ped) stitch
sm	small
sp	space
ssk	slip, slip, knit
ssp	slip, slip, purl
st(s)	stitch(es)
St st	stockinette stitch
TB	twist back
tbl	through back of loop(s)
t-ch	turning chain
TF	twist front
tog	together
tr	treble (crochet)
wpi	wraps per inch
WS	wrong side
wyib	with yarn in back
wyif	with yarn in front
yb; ybk	yarn at back
yd(s)	yard(s)
yf; yfwd	yarn forward
yo	yarn over
yo2	yarn over twice
yrn	yarn around needle
*	repeat starting point
**	same as *, but used to separate * instructions from the new instructions
()	alternate measurements and/or instructions
[]	instructions that are to be worked as a group the specified number of times

CONTINUED ON NEXT PAGE

KNITTING TERMS

A

as established   Work in a particular pattern, as previously set.

as foll   Work as the instructions direct below.

as if to knit   Knitwise; insert the needle into the stitch the same way you would if you were knitting it.

as if to purl   Purlwise; insert the needle into the stitch the same way you would if you were purling it.

at the same time   Work more than one set of instructions simultaneously.

axis stitch   The center stitch between two increases or decreases.

B

bind off in patt   Work stitch pattern while binding off.

bind off loosely   Bind off without pulling the working yarn too tight, so that the finished edge is elastic.

block   Lay knit pieces out flat and dampen or steam them to form them to the proper shape and measurements.

C

change to larger needles   Use the larger needles specified in the pattern, starting with the next row.

change to smaller needles   Use the smaller needles specified in the pattern, starting with the next row.

E

ending with a RS row   Work a right side row as the last row you work.

ending with a WS row   Work a wrong side row as the last row you work.

every other row   Work as instructed on alternate rows only.

F

fasten off   At the end of a bind-off, pull the yarn through the last stitch and tighten.

from beg   From the cast-on edge; usually used to direct where to start measuring a knitted piece.

J

join round   When knitting in the round, work the first stitch of the round so that the last stitch and the first stitch join, forming a circle.

K

knitwise   As if to knit; insert the needle into the stitch the same way you would if you were knitting it.

L

lower edge   Cast-on edge.

M

marker   Something used to mark a point in a stitch pattern or to mark a point in your knitting, be it a plastic ring stitch marker, safety pin, or tied piece of yarn.

multiple   The number of stitches necessary to achieve one pattern repeat.

P

pick up and knit   A method of picking up stitches, as for a collar or button band, where the knitting needle is inserted into the work, yarn is wrapped around the needle as if to knit, and the new loop is pulled through.

place marker   Slip a stitch marker onto the knitting needle to indicate special instructions regarding the stitch following; or place some other sort of marker, such as a safety pin or strand of yarn, to indicate where buttons will be.

purlwise   As if to purl; insert the needle into the stitch the same way you would if you were purling it.

R

reverse shaping   When working something like a cardigan, where the fronts are mirror images of each other, instructions for shaping are given for one front; you need to reverse those instructions for shaping the other front.

right side (RS)   The side of the knitting that will show.

S

selvage   An extra stitch (or stitches) that will be used for the seam.

slip stitches to holder   Put the stitches onto a stitch holder, usually to be worked later.

T

turning ridge   A row of stitches, usually purled on the right side of stockinette stitch, where a hem will be folded under.

W

weave in ends   When finishing a project, sew loose ends in and out of the backs of stitches or into seams to prevent them from unraveling.

with RS facing   Work with the right side facing you; usually used when instructions are telling you to pick up stitches for a button band or collar.

with WS facing   Work with the wrong side facing you.

work across   Continue to work as established across the row of stitches or across a group of stitches on a holder.

work buttonholes opposite markers   When working the fronts of a cardigan, place markers on the side where the buttons will be sewn and work buttonholes on the other front, opposite the markers.

work even   Work without increasing or decreasing.

work to end   Finish the row.

working needle   The needle that is being used to knit or purl stitches.

working yarn   The yarn that is being used to knit or purl stitches.

wrong side (WS)   The side of the knitting that will not show.

A knitting pattern contains all the information you need to make a certain design. In addition to the instructions, a pattern should list what sizes the design can be knit for, the tools and materials required, and any particular stitch patterns used. Some patterns also contain diagrams of the finished pieces, called *schematics*, which show the shape of the pieces and their measurements.

READING THE PATTERN FIRST

There are so many knitting patterns and books to choose from these days that you may be overwhelmed. When you find something that you would like to knit, be sure to read over the pattern first. Check to see that the instructions are clear and that they make sense to you. Make sure that the pattern is within your skill level. Many patterns are rated, ranging from very easy to expert. If the pattern isn't rated, reading it over will let you know if it's something you can handle. Trying to knit something that is too difficult may turn you off to knitting forever, and you certainly don't want that. Also, you need to make certain that the instructions are written for a size that you would like to knit.

What Size to Knit?					
Actual Body Measurement	*Finished Measurements*				
Chest	*Tight Fit*	*Tailored Fit*	*Normal Fit*	*Loose Fit*	*Oversized Fit*
31"–32"	30"	32"	34"	36"	37"–38"
33"–34"	32"	34"	36"	38"	39"–40"
35"–36"	34"	36"	38"	40"	41"–42"
37"–38"	36"	38"	40"	42"	43"–44"
39"–40"	38"	40"	42"	44"	45"–46"

READING INSTRUCTIONS FOR SIZE

Most knitting patterns are written for more than one size. The smallest size is usually listed first, with the remaining sizes listed in parentheses—for example, S (M, L). Throughout the pattern, the instructions contain information pertaining to the various sizes, such as stitch counts and numbers of decreases or increases, using a parallel format. For example, a pattern written for S (M, L) may instruct you to cast on 50 (60, 70) stitches. That means if you're knitting the medium size, you need to cast on 60 stitches. Some knitters avoid confusion by highlighting or underlining the part of the instructions that pertain to the size they are knitting.

CHOOSING A SIZE

Knitting patterns list the measurements relating to the sizes included in the instructions. These measurements usually indicate the finished sizes of the knitted garment. Different designers use unique templates based on their idea of what fits a certain age or size range. So the best way to figure out what size to knit for yourself or for someone else is, if possible, to take body measurements. Then you can decide whether you want the garment to have a loose, comfortable fit, or a more snug, tailored fit. You then check your measurements against the pattern's finished measurements and make your choice.

TAKING BODY MEASUREMENTS

To take body measurements, you need a tape measure. Measure the bust or chest by placing the tape measure around the fullest part of the chest, at the underarm. For the waist, measure around the smallest part of the torso. For the hip, measure around the fullest part of the lower torso. Measure for the sleeve length by placing the tape measure at the edge of the shoulder and extending down (with arm held straight at side) to the wrist. Also measure from the underarm to the wrist to obtain a measurement for where to begin the sleeve cap shaping. Some of your knitted measurements should be a few inches larger than the actual body measurements, or the garment will be too tight. If the garment is very tailored, you may want to also measure the circumference of the upper arms, wrists, and neck.

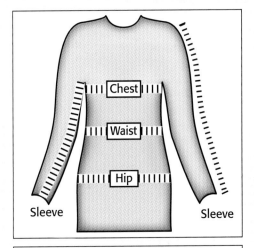

READING SCHEMATICS

Schematics are diagrams of the finished knit pieces for a project. They indicate the measurements for each piece before everything has been sewn together. Schematics are a very handy reference: You can measure your knitting as you go along and compare it to the schematics to make sure you're coming up with the same thing. Or if your row gauge is slightly off, you can follow the schematic instead of the instructions' row counts to make certain your pieces will be the correct length. Note, however, that the measurements listed on schematics do not include embellishments such as collars, button bands, or decorative edgings that are added later.

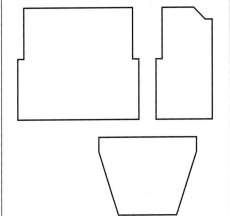

GATHERING MATERIALS AND TOOLS

A knitting pattern lists the materials and tools you need to complete the project. Some knitting patterns specify a number of balls of a particular brand of yarn. If you plan to substitute, be sure to purchase the same number of *yards* of a yarn that knits to the same gauge—not just the same total weight of yarn. Some patterns simply specify a number of yards of a particular weight yarn. Either way, it's not a bad idea to buy an extra ball, just in case. A pattern usually also lists needle types and sizes, as well as any special tools you need. It's a good idea to gather all these materials before starting. However, you may want to wait until you have sewn your sweater together before purchasing buttons or other fasteners.

At some point, you will come across a stitch chart or color chart on a knitting pattern, particularly if the design employs color work, textured stitches, or cables. Don't be intimidated by all the symbols and hieroglyphics you see there; most patterns provide a key to all the symbols used in each chart.

READING A CHART IN THE RIGHT DIRECTION

A square of a knitting chart represents a stitch; a horizontal row of squares represents a row. You read a chart as you work the knitting: from bottom to top and starting at the lower-right corner. The first horizontal row of squares represents a right side row (unless otherwise specified) and is read from right to left. The second horizontal row, a wrong side row, is read from left to right. (For circular knitting, all chart rows are read from right to left.) Most charts represent only a partial section of the knitting that is repeated to create the overall pattern. So, after you work the last stitch in a chart row, you return to the beginning of the same chart row and repeat. Working row-wise is the same: After you work the last row of the chart, you repeat the chart from the bottom.

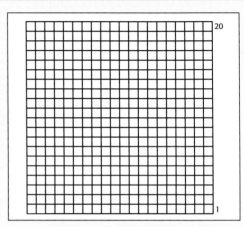

READING A COLOR CHART

When a chart is used to represent a color pattern, each square is filled with a particular color or a symbol that corresponds with the color of yarn in which that stitch and/or row should be worked. You read this type of chart as described above: from bottom to top and back and forth, starting with the lower-right corner.

READING A STITCH PATTERN CHART

When a chart is used to represent a textured stitch pattern, each square is either empty or contains a symbol. Symbols vary from pattern to pattern. For simple knit and purl patterns, an empty square means "knit on the right side rows and purl on the wrong side rows." A square that contains a dot means "purl on the right side rows and knit on the wrong side rows." More complex stitch patterns, such as cable patterns, for example, contain many symbols representing different techniques.

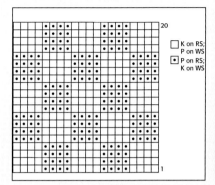

☐ K on RS; P on WS
☑ P on RS; K on WS

COMMON SYMBOLS USED IN KNITTING CHARTS

Symbol charts employ a language of symbols to convey instructions relating to a particular stitch or group of stitches. Unfortunately, these symbols vary from one designer to another—particularly symbols for cable stitches—so use the key to the symbols they provide. All good patterns include clear written instructions along with the chart, so don't feel you have to learn symbols by heart. The following table shows a number of knitting chart symbols you might encounter.

	Common Knitting Chart Symbols	
Symbol	**Meaning**	
	K on RS; P on WS	
●	P on RS; K on WS	
O	Yarn over (yo)	
∨	Slip st as if to knit, with yarn in back on RS; slip stitch as if to knit, with yarn in front on WS	
⊻	Slip st as if to purl, with yarn in back on RS; slip stitch as if to purl, with yarn in front on WS	
⋈	Perform make one (M1) increase	
⋏	Knit 2 stitches together (k2tog)	
⋏	Purl 2 stitches together (p2tog)	
⋏	Knit 3 stitches together (k3tog) on RS; purl 3 stitches together (p3tog) on WS	
⋏	Purl 3 stitches together (p3tog) on RS; knit 3 stitches together (k3tog) on WS	
⋋	Slip 1, knit 1, pass slipped stitch over knit stitch (skp)	
⋌	Slip, slip, knit (ssk)	
●	Make bobble (mb)	

chapter 7

Knitting in the Round

Knitting in the round, or *circular knitting*, is what you do when you want to knit a tube. Hats, socks, mittens, gloves, and skirts are frequently knit in the round. When you knit in the round, you knit around and around on the right side only. So if you're working in stockinette stitch, knitting in the round eliminates the need to purl. It also reduces the necessity of sewing seams.

Cast On with Circular Needles

Circular needles are basically needle tips connected by a plastic or nylon cord. Used mainly for knitting tubular items, they come in a variety of materials and lengths. Whether you use wood, metal, or plastic is up to you. The circumference of what you are going to knit determines what length needle you can use, and your pattern will specify the length. The key to casting on to a circular needle is ensuring that the stitches do not get twisted.

How to Cast On with Circular Needles

If the cord on your circular needle is very curly and hard to manage, try immersing it in hot water for a minute or two, and then straighten it. It will be much easier to work with.

1 Cast on stitches in the same manner you would with straight needles, using the method of your choice.

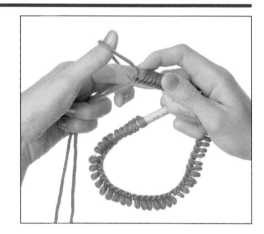

2 When you have cast on the correct number of stitches, make sure that your stitches are not twisted.

Note: To avoid twisted stitches, make sure the cast-on edge is going around the inside of the needle.

Knit Using Circular Needles

When you knit on circular needles, you knit in *rounds,* not rows. Every round is a right side row, so if you're working in stockinette stitch, you do not have to purl.

Take care not to let the stitches get twisted before joining your round. If they are twisted and you knit a few rounds, the entire piece of knitting will be twisted. The only way to correct this is to unravel all the way back to the cast-on row.

How to Knit on Circular Needles

1 Hold the end of the needle that the working yarn is attached to in your right hand. Place a stitch marker after the last stitch that was cast on to mark the end of the round.

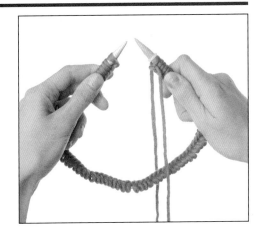

2 Use the needle in your right hand to knit the first cast-on stitch from the needle in your left hand, giving the yarn a firm tug (on this first stitch only) so that the join is snug.

Knitting the first stitch joins the round.

3 Knit all the way around until you reach the stitch marker. To begin the second round, slip the marker from the left needle to the right needle and knit the first stitch as in step 2.

Cast On with Double-Pointed Needles

Before circular needles were invented, circular knitting was done on double-pointed needles. Today, double-pointed needles are used mainly for smaller items, like hats and socks. They are sold in sets of four or five. You need four for this lesson.

Casting on with double-pointed needles is similar to casting on with circular needles in that you must avoid twisting the stitches. The difference is that you spread the cast-on stitches over three needles.

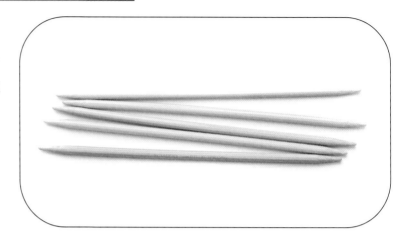

How to Cast On with Double-Pointed Needles

① Cast on all the stitches called for onto one double-pointed needle. Then slip one-third of the stitches onto a second needle and one-third onto a third needle.

Note: *If the stitches can't be divided equally in thirds, be approximate.*

② Arrange the three needles so that they form a triangle: The needle with the working yarn attached should be the right side of the triangle (a), the center needle should be the base of the triangle (b), and the needle with the first cast-on stitch should be the left side of the triangle (c).

Note: *Make sure the cast-on edge is running around the center of the triangle, untwisted.*

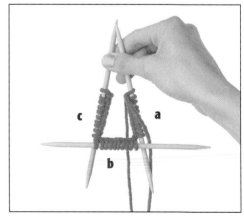

Knitting on double-pointed needles can feel awkward at first, but once you work a few rounds, it will all come together. It is really the best way to knit mittens and gloves, so it's worth giving this type of knitting a try.

How to Knit on Double-Pointed Needles

1 Make sure the needles are facing you, with the needle with the working yarn attached to it on the right. Place a stitch marker after the last stitch that was cast on to mark the end of the round. Hold the needle with the first cast-on stitch on it in your left hand.

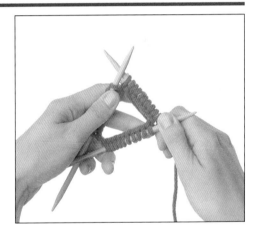

2 Using your fourth needle, join the round by knitting the first cast-on stitch from the left needle, giving the yarn a firm tug (on this first stitch only) so that the join is snug.

Knitting the first stitch joins the round.

3 Knit all the way around until you reach the stitch marker. To begin the second round, slip the marker from the left needle to the right needle and knit the first stitch as in step 2.

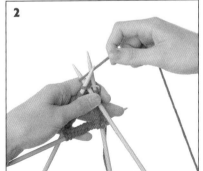

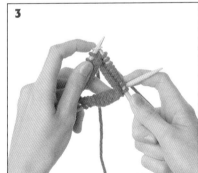

More Complicated Stitch Patterns: Bobbles, Knots, and Cables

This chapter covers the more advanced stitch treatments you need to know to make a highly textured sweater: bobbles, knots, and cables. Most cable work involves holding a stitch or stitches on a cable needle, working the next stitch or few, and then working the stitches from the cable needle. Simple cables are easy to do and can add a sculptural accent to your knitting. Included here are a variety of bobble stitches, knot stitches, and cables. Experiment with some of the combinations here and then see if you can create your own.

Knit with Bobbles and Knots

Bobbles and knots add an exciting three-dimensional quality to your knitting. Bobbles and knots can be used for effect in many ways: as a single row along a border, repeated in an allover pattern, or placed inside cables. Different designers make bobbles in different ways; you should find the way that suits you best.

Bobble Stitches

HOW TO MAKE A BOBBLE

Many bobble-making methods involve knitting several times into one stitch, turning the work and working the new stitches, and then turning it back again. The method shown here is easy and doesn't require turning. The abbreviation for make a bobble is mb.

1. Work to the point where you want the bobble. Knit into the front, back, front, back, and front (that's five times) of the next stitch.

2. Without turning work, use the left needle to pick up the fourth stitch and pass it over the fifth and off the needle; pass the third stitch over the fifth and off the needle; pass the second stitch over the fifth and off the needle; and finally, pass the first stitch over the fifth and off the needle.

   Knitting five times into 1 stitch and then passing the 4 extra stitches, one at a time, over the last stitch forms a bobble.

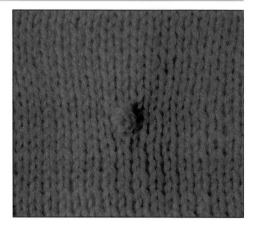

BOBBLE STITCH

Here's a pattern that is similar to simple seed stitch (page 37), except on right side rows you work a bobble (as described above) where the purl stitch would be. You work this pattern on a multiple of 4 stitches plus 3.

1. Row 1 (RS–bobble row): *K3, make bobble (mb); repeat from * to last 3 stitches, k3.

2. Rows 2, 4, and 6: Purl.

3. Rows 3 and 5: Knit.

4. Row 7 (bobble row): K1, mb, *k3, mb; repeat from * to last stitch, k1.

5. Rows 8, 10, and 12: Purl.

6. Rows 9 and 11: Knit.

7. Repeat rows 1–12 for bobble stitch.

TRINITY STITCH

Trinity stitch, which is also referred to as *bramble stitch*, works very well alongside cable panels. You work it on a multiple of 4 stitches plus 2.

1. Row 1 (RS): Purl.

2. Row 2 (WS): K1, *[k1, p1, k1] into the next stitch, p3tog ; repeat from * to last stitch, k1.

3. Row 3: Purl.

4. Row 4: K1, *p3tog, [k1, p1, k1] into the next stitch; repeat from * to last stitch, k1.

5. Repeat rows 1–4 for trinity stitch.

Knot Stitches

KNOT STITCH

This is a textured stitch pattern that works well for sweaters, jackets, and bags. You work it over a multiple of 2 stitches plus 1.

1. Row 1 (RS): Knit.

2. Row 2 (WS): K1, *p2tog without slipping stitches off the needle, bring yarn to back and knit the same 2 stitches together; repeat from * to end.

3. Row 3: Knit.

4. Row 4: *P2tog without slipping stitches off the needle, bring yarn to back and knit the same 2 stitches together; repeat from * to last stitch, k1.

5. Repeat rows 1–4 for knot stitch.

PILLARED KNOT STITCH

This interesting pattern resembles a rib, and it does pull in like a rib but without a lot of elasticity. You work it over a multiple of 4 stitches plus 1.

1. Row 1 (RS): K1, *p3tog without slipping stitches from the left needle, bring yarn to back and knit the same 3 stitches together without slipping stitches from the left needle, bring yarn back to the front and purl the 3 stitches together, k1; repeat from * to end.

2. Row 2 (WS): Purl.

3. Repeat rows 1 and 2 for pillared knot stitch.

Make Simple Cables

Cables look more complicated than they actually are. If you can knit, purl, put stitches on a holder, and count, you can make a simple cable.

You make basic cables by holding one or more stitches on a cable needle to the front or the back of your work, knitting the next one or more stitches from the left needle, and then knitting the stitches from the cable needle. Whether you hold the stitches to the back or front determines which direction the cable crosses.

Simple Back Cross Cable

To practice making a cable, you need needles, yarn, a row counter, and a cable needle. Cast on 16 stitches and then work rows 1 and 2 shown below to set up for the cables. Your cable will be worked on the 6 stitches at the center, with 5 stitches of reverse stockinette stitch on either side. Remember to click your row counter ahead each time you complete a row.

① Row 1 (RS): P5, k6, p5.

② Row 2 (WS): K5, p6, k5.

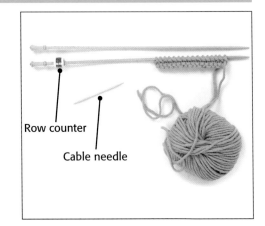

Row counter

Cable needle

③ Row 3 (cable row): P5, slip the next 3 stitches to a cable needle as if to purl and hold at back of work (a). Knit the next 3 stitches from the left needle. Now use the right needle to knit the 3 stitches from the cable needle, starting with the first stitch that was slipped onto the needle (b), p5.

④ Row 4: Repeat row 2.

⑤ Repeat rows 1–4 for back cross, or right, cable.

Note: If knitting from the cable needle feels awkward, try slipping the held stitches back to the left needle, without twisting, before knitting them.

Simple Front Cross Cable

Making a front cross cable will be easy now that you have done the back cross cable. The only difference is that for this cable, you hold the stitches on the cable needle to the front of your work. You need to cast on 16 stitches, as before.

a

① Row 1 (RS): P5, k6, p5.

② Row 2 (WS): K5, p6, k5.

③ Row 3 (cable row): P5, slip the next 3 stitches to a cable needle as if to purl and hold at front of work (a). Knit the next 3 stitches from the left needle. Now use the right needle to knit the 3 stitches from the cable needle, starting with the first stitch that was slipped onto the needle (b), p5.

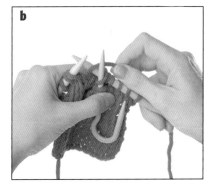
b

④ Row 4: Repeat row 2.

⑤ Repeat rows 1–4 for front cross, or left, cable.

FAQ

I have noticed that there are different sizes and types of cable needles. Which one should I chose?

In terms of size, you should always use a cable needle that is slightly smaller in diameter than your working knitting needle. If you use one that is too thick, you will stretch out your stitches. The type of cable needle you choose depends entirely on your preference. A lot of knitters choose one that looks like a tiny double-pointed needle because it's easier to knit directly from it. Others prefer a hook-shaped cable needle because the stitches don't fall off it very easily, and it hangs down out of the way when knitting the other stitches. Borrow the various types from knitting friends and try them out so that you can find the style that suits you best.

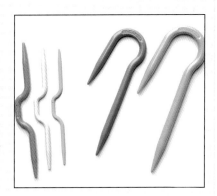

Now that you have seen how you can move stitches and cross them in your knitting, you are ready to try some other cable patterns.

Most instructions for cable knit garments break down the various stitch patterns and cable elements into panels so that they're easier to follow. The following cable panels include 2 stitches in reverse stockinette stitch on each side of the cable.

More Cable Patterns

BRAIDED CABLE (12-STITCH PANEL)

This cable is easier to make than it looks.

1 Row 1 (RS–cable row): P2, *slip the next 2 stitches to a cable needle and hold at back, knit the next 2 stitches from the left needle, knit the 2 stitches from the cable needle; repeat from * to last 2 stitches, p2.

2 Row 2 (WS): K2, p8, k2.

3 Row 3 (cable row): P2, k2, slip the next 2 stitches to a cable needle and hold at front, knit the next 2 stitches from the left needle, k2 stitches from the cable needle, k2, p2.

4 Row 4: Repeat row 2.

5 Repeat rows 1–4 for braided cable.

WAVE CABLE (10-STITCH PANEL)

This cable is similar to the cables you made earlier, except that you perform both the front cross and back cross in the same cable.

1 Row 1 (RS): P2, k6, p2.

2 Row 2 (WS): K2, p6, k2.

3 Row 3 (cable row): P2, slip the next 3 stitches to a cable needle and hold at back, knit the next 3 stitches from the left needle, knit the 3 stitches from the cable needle, p2.

4 Row 4: Repeat row 2.

5 Rows 5–8: Repeat rows 1 and 2 twice.

6 Row 9 (cable row): P2, slip the next 3 stitches to a cable needle and hold at front, knit the next 3 stitches from the left needle, knit the 3 stitches from the cable needle, p2.

7 Rows 10 and 12: Repeat row 2.

8 Row 11: Repeat row 1.

9 Repeat rows 1–12 for wave cable.

DOUBLE CABLE (12-STITCH PANEL)

You can make this cable so that it looks like it's pointing upward or downward.

1 Row 1 (RS): P2, k8, p2.

2 Row 2 (WS): K2, p8, k2.

3 Row 3 (cable row): P2, slip the next 2 stitches to a cable needle and hold at front, knit the next 2 stitches from the left needle, knit the 2 stitches from the cable needle; slip the next 2 stitches to a cable needle and hold at back, knit the next 2 stitches from the left needle, k2 stitches from the cable needle; p2.

4 Row 4: Repeat row 2.

5 Rows 5–8: Repeat rows 1 and 2 twice.

6 Repeat rows 1–8 for double cable.

Note: To make the cable point upward, work all rows the same, except on row 3 reverse the order of the front and back crosses.

Upward cable   Downward cable

CONTINUED ON NEXT PAGE

HONEYCOMB CABLE (20-STITCH PANEL)

You can widen this interesting cable by adding multiples of 8 stitches.

1 Row 1 (RS–cable row): P2, *slip the next 2 stitches to a cable needle and hold at back, knit the next 2 stitches from the left needle, knit the 2 stitches from the cable needle; slip the next 2 stitches to a cable needle and hold at front, knit the next 2 stitches from the left needle, knit the 2 stitches from the cable needle; repeat from * to last 2 stitches, p2.

2 Rows 2, 4, 6, and 8 (WS): K2, p16, k2.

3 Rows 3 and 7: P2, k16, p2.

4 Row 5 (cable row): P2, *slip the next 2 stitches to a cable needle and hold at front, knit the next 2 stitches from the left needle, knit the 2 stitches from the cable needle; slip the next 2 stitches to a cable needle and hold at back, knit the next 2 stitches from the left needle, knit the 2 stitches from the cable needle; repeat from * to last 2 stitches, p2.

5 Repeat rows 1–8 for honeycomb cable.

GARTER AND STOCKINETTE STITCH CABLE (14-STITCH PANEL)

Here's a pretty cable that you don't see very often.

1 Row 1 (RS): P2, k10, p2.

2 Row 2 (WS): K2, p5, k7.

3 Rows 3–6: Repeat rows 1 and 2 twice.

4 Row 7 (cable row): P2, slip the next 5 stitches to a cable needle and hold at back, knit the next 5 stitches from the left needle, knit stitches from the cable needle, p2.

5 Row 8: K7, p5, k2.

6 Row 9: Repeat row 1.

7 Rows 10–16: Repeat rows 8 and 9 three more times; then repeat row 8 once more.

8 Row 17 (cable row): Repeat row 7.

9 Row 18: Repeat row 2.

10 Row 19: Repeat row 1.

11 Rows 20–22: Repeat rows 18 and 19 once; then repeat row 18 once more.

12 Repeat rows 1–22 for garter and stockinette stitch cable.

Combine Cables with Bobbles, Knots, and Textured Stitches

Here are a few cables that integrate bobbles, knots, or textured stitches into their structure. Most of these combinations take on an embossed, or sculptural, quality, which is what is so fascinating about knitting with cables.

Fancy Cable Stitches

KNOTTED CABLE (10-STITCH PANEL)

This cable involves moving the cable needle from front to back and working the held stitches in stages.

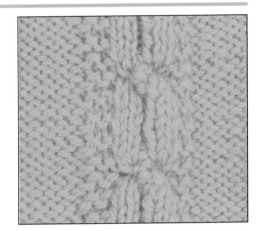

1. Rows 1, 5, 7, and 9 (RS): P2, k2, p2, k2, p2.

2. Rows 2, 4, 6, and 8, and 10 (WS): P4, k2, p4.

3. Row 3 (cable row): P2, slip the next 4 stitches to a cable needle and hold at the front, knit the next 2 stitches from the left needle; then slip 2 stitches from the cable needle back to the left needle. Bring the cable needle (with the remaining 2 stitches on it) to the back, purl the 2 stitches that were moved back to the left needle; knit the 2 stitches from the cable needle, p2.

4. Repeat rows 1–10 for knotted cable.

CONTINUED ON NEXT PAGE

BOBBLE CABLE (13-STITCH PANEL)

This cable uses the following abbreviations:

mb (make bobble): For a refresher on how to make a bobble, see page 96.

T3B: Slip the next stitch to a cable needle and hold at back, k2 from the left needle, p1 from the cable needle.

T3F: Slip the next 2 stitches to a cable needle and hold at front, p1 from the left needle, k2 from the cable needle.

1. Row 1 (RS—cable row): P3, T3B, p1, T3F, p3.
2. Rows 2 and 8 (WS): K3, p2, k3, p2, k3.
3. Row 3 (cable row): P2, T3B, p3, T3F, p2.
4. Rows 4 and 6: K2, p2, k5, p2, k2.
5. Row 5 (bobble row): P2, k2, p2, mb, p2, k2, p2.
6. Row 7 (cable row): P2, T3F, p3, T3B, p2.
7. Row 9 (cable row): P3, T3F, p1, T3B, p3.
8. Rows 10 and 12: K4, p5, k4.
9. Row 11 (cable row): P4, slip the next 3 stitches to a cable needle and hold at back, knit the next 2 stitches from the left needle, then p1, k2 from the cable needle, p4.
10. Repeat rows 1–12 for bobble cable.

RIBBED CABLE (15-STITCH PANEL)

Here's a cable that is worked in k1, p1 ribbing.

1. Row 1 (RS): P2, k1, *p1, k1; repeat from * four times to last 2 stitches, p2.
2. Row 2 (WS): K2, purl into back of next stitch, *k1, purl into back of next stitch; repeat from * four times to last 2 stitches, k2.
3. Row 3 (cable row): P2, slip the next 6 stitches to a cable needle and hold at back, k1, [p1, k1] twice from the left needle, then [p1, k1] three times from the cable needle; p2.
4. Row 4: Repeat row 2.
5. Rows 5–14: Repeat rows 1 and 2 five times.
6. Repeat rows 1–14 for ribbed cable.

WISHBONE AND SEED STITCH CABLE (12-STITCH PANEL)

This is a delicate cable that looks complicated but is easy to do.

1 Row 1 (RS–cable row): P2, slip the next 3 stitches to a cable needle and hold at back, k1, [p1, k1, p1] from the cable needle; slip the next stitch to a cable needle and hold at front, [k1, p1, k1], k1 from the cable needle; p2.

2 Rows 2, 4, and 6 (WS): K2, *p1, k1; repeat from * twice, p2, k2.

3 Rows 3 and 5: P2, *knit 1, p1; repeat from * twice, k2, p2.

4 Row 7: P2, k1, p1, k3, p1, k2, p2.

5 Row 8: K2, p1, k1, p3, k1, p2, k2.

6 Repeat rows 1–8 for wishbone and seed stitch cable.

HOLLOW OAK CABLE (15-STITCH PANEL)

This cable uses the following abbreviations:

mb (make bobble): For a refresher on how to make a bobble, see page 96.

T3B: Slip the next stitch to a cable needle and hold at back, k2 from the left needle, p1 from the cable needle.

T3F: Slip the next 2 stitches to a cable needle and hold at front, p1 from the left needle, k2 from the cable needle.

1 Rows 1 and 5 (RS–bobble row): P5, k2, mb, k2, p5.

2 Rows 2, 4, 6, and 20 (WS): K5, p5, k5.

3 Row 3 (bobble row): P5, mb, k3, mb, p5.

4 Row 7 (cable row): P4, T3B, p1, T3F, p4.

5 Row 8: K4, p2, k1, p1, k1, p2, k4.

6 Row 9 (cable row): P3, T3B, k1, p1, k1, T3F, p3.

7 Row 10: K3, p3, k1, p1, k1, p3, k3.

8 Row 11 (cable row): P2, T3B, [p1, k1] twice, p1, T3F, p2.

9 Row 12: K2, p2, [k1, p1] three times, k1, p2, k2.

10 Row 13: P2, k3, [p1, k1] twice, p1, k3, p2.

11 Rows 14, 16, and 18: Repeat rows 12, 10, and 8, respectively.

12 Row 15 (cable row): P2, T3F, [p1, k1] twice, p1, T3B, p2.

13 Row 17 (cable row): P3, T3F, k1, p1, k1, T3B, p3.

14 Row 19 (cable row): P4, T3F, p1, T3B, p4.

15 Repeat rows 1–20 for hollow oak cable.

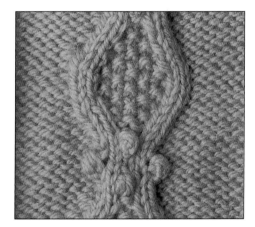

Openwork

Remember the yarn over stitch from Chapter 3? That simple act of bringing the yarn over the needle to create a new stitch—and at the same time a hole—can create beautiful and elaborate lace and openwork patterns when repeated at various intervals in your knitting.

Learn Drop Stitch and Yarn Over Patterns

Most drop stitch patterns involve performing a yarn over two or more times in the same place across the row. When you work the next row, you knit across, dropping the yarn overs from the needle, and this results in a band of mesh-like vertical strands between regular rows. Yarn over patterns employ yarn overs in conjunction with decreases in various configurations, resulting in a broad range of openwork fabrics.

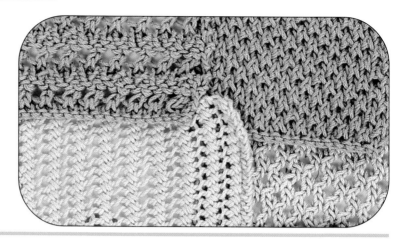

Drop Stitch Patterns

DROP STITCH GARTER PATTERN

This is an easy drop stitch pattern that makes wonderful scarves, throws, and shawls. You can work it on any number of stitches.

1. Row 1 (RS): Knit.
2. Row 2 (WS): Knit.
3. Row 3: K1, *yo twice, k1; repeat from * to end.
4. Row 4: Knit across, dropping the yo loops as you go.
5. Repeat rows 1–4 for drop stitch garter pattern.

SEAFOAM PATTERN

This drop stitch pattern is great for scarves, wraps, shawls, and baby blankets. You work it on a multiple of 10 stitches plus 6.

1. Row 1 (RS): Knit.
2. Row 2 (WS): Knit.
3. Row 3: K6, *yo twice, k1, yo three times, k1, yo four times, k1, yo three times, k1, yo twice, k6; repeat from * to end.
4. Rows 4 and 8: Knit across, dropping the yo loops as you go.
5. Rows 5 and 6: Knit.
6. Row 7: K1, *yo twice, k1, yo three times, k1, yo four times, k1, yo three times, k1, yo twice, k6; repeat from * across, but end last repeat with k1.
7. Repeat rows 1–8 for seafoam pattern.

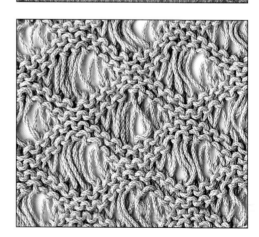

YARN OVER STRIPE PATTERN

This is an easy openwork pattern that repeats as a horizontal stripe. You work it on an even number of stitches.

1. Row 1 (RS): K1, *yo, k1; repeat from * to last stitch, k1.

2. Row 2 (WS): K1, purl across to last stitch, k1.

3. Row 3: K1, *k2tog; repeat from * to last stitch, k1.

4. Rows 4 and 5: K1, *yo, k2tog; repeat from * to last stitch, k1.

5. Row 6: Knit.

6. Repeat rows 1–6 for yarn over stripe pattern.

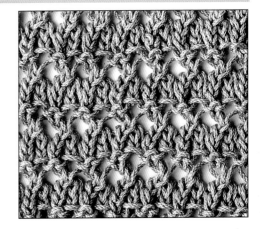

MESH PATTERN

This is an easy and versatile pattern that combines a yarn over with a slip 1, knit 1, pass slipped stitch over, abbreviated skp. (For a refresher on skp, see page 57.) It looks great in both fine and bulky yarns. You work it on an even number of stitches.

1. Row 1 (RS): K1, *yo, slip 1, k1, psso; repeat from * to last stitch, k1.

2. Row 2 (WS): Repeat row 1.

3. Repeat rows 1 and 2 for mesh pattern.

BRIOCHE HONEYCOMB PATTERN

Brioche patterns combine yarn overs with slipped stitches and knit 2 togethers (or purl 2 togethers), and the result is usually a loose but three-dimensional fabric. Going up a needle size gives this a nice, soft drape. You work it on an even number of stitches.

1. Row 1 (WS): *Yo, slip 1 with yarn at back, k1; repeat from * to end.

2. Row 2 (RS): *K1, k2tog (these will be the yo and the slipped stitch from the row before); repeat from * to end.

3. Row 3: K1, *yo, slip 1 with yarn at back, k1; repeat from * to last stitch, k1.

4. Row 4: K2, *k2tog, k1; repeat from * to end.

5. Repeat rows 1–4 for brioche honeycomb pattern.

Experiment with Eyelet Patterns

Eyelets are the little holes that are created by combining a yarn over with a knit 2 together. Eyelet patterns usually have more knitted fabric between the holes than lace patterns, and they are therefore less open. Eyelet patterns generally add a delicate touch, suitable for baby clothes, elegant spring sweaters, or little girls' dresses.

Eyelet Patterns

CELL STITCH

This is an easy and very open eyelet pattern. It makes great scarves and throws. Note that the first row is a wrong side row. You work this stitch on a multiple of 3 stitches.

1 Rows 1 and 3 (WS): Purl.

2 Row 2 (RS): K2, *k2tog, yo, k1; repeat from * to last stitch, k1.

3 Row 4: K2, *yo, k1, k2tog; repeat from * to last stitch, k1.

4 Repeat rows 1–4 for cell stitch.

EYELET CHEVRONS

This pattern uses a slip 1, knit 1, pass slipped stitch over, abbreviated skp. You work it on a multiple of 9 stitches.

1 Row 1 (RS): *K4, yo, skp, k3; repeat from * to end.

2 Rows 2, 4, 6, and 8 (WS): Purl.

3 Row 3: *K2, k2tog, yo, k1, yo, skp, k2; repeat from * to end.

4 Row 5: *K1, k2tog, yo, k3, yo, skp, k1; repeat from * to end.

5 Row 7: *K2tog, yo, k5, yo, skp; repeat from * to end.

6 Repeat rows 1–8 for eyelet chevrons.

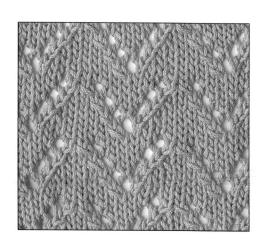

FALLING RAIN PATTERN

This eyelet pattern is worked on a background of reverse stockinette stitch. You work it on a multiple of 6 stitches.

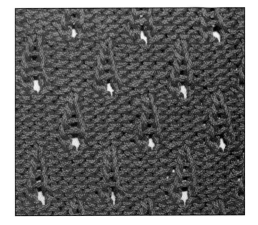

1 Row 1 (RS): *P4, yo, p2tog*; repeat from * to end.

2 Rows 2, 4, and 6 (WS): K1, *p1, k5; repeat from * to last 5 stitches, p1, k4.

3 Rows 3 and 5: P4, *k1, p5; repeat from * to last 2 stitches, k1, p1.

4 Row 7: P1, *yo, p2tog, p4; repeat from * to last 5 stitches, yo, p2tog, p3.

5 Rows 8, 10, and 12: K4, *p1, k5; repeat from * to last 2 stitches, p1, k1.

6 Rows 9 and 11: P1, *k1, p5; repeat from * to last 5 stitches, k1, p4.

Repeat rows 1–12 for falling rain pattern.

WINDOW EYELETS

This pattern combines yarn overs with knit 3 togethers to create a design that looks like a grid of window panes. You work this pattern on a multiple of 4 stitches plus 3.

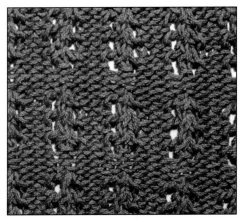

1 Rows 1 and 3 (WS): Knit.

2 Row 2 (RS): Purl.

3 Row 4: P3, *yo, k1, yo, p3; repeat from * to end.

4 Rows 5, 7, and 9: K3, *p3, k3; repeat from * to end.

5 Rows 6 and 8: P3, *yo, k3tog, yo, p3; repeat from * to end.

6 Row 10: P3, *k3tog, p3; repeat from * to end.

7 Repeat rows 1–10 for window eyelets.

SNOWFLAKE BAND

This eyelet pattern works well as a decorative border along a hem or cuff, or it can be repeated as an allover pattern. It uses a decrease called pass 2 slipped stitches over (p2sso). P2sso is like a slip 1, knit 1, psso—or skp—except you slip 2 stitches instead of 1, and you pass the 2 slipped stitches, instead of 1, over the knit stitch. You work this pattern on a multiple of 7 stitches.

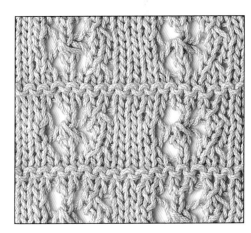

1 Row 1 (WS): Knit.

2 Rows 2 and 10 (RS): Knit.

3 Rows 3, 5, 7, and 9: Purl.

4 Rows 4 and 8: K4, *k2tog, yo, k1, yo, k2tog, k3; repeat from * to last stitch, k1.

5 Row 6: K5, *yo, slip 2, k1, p2sso, yo, k5; repeat from * to end.

6 Repeat rows 1–10 for snowflake band.

Work with Lace Patterns

Lace patterns, like eyelet patterns, are generally somewhat dainty and elegant. Lace appears in all kinds of designs—fancy sweaters, shawls, throws, tablecloths, and as decorative borders. It's a wonder to watch your pattern develop row by row.

Lace Patterns

LACE RIB

This pattern uses the decrease slip, slip, knit, abbreviated ssk. (For a refresher on ssk, see page 56.) Also called faggoting, this lace is worked on a multiple of 3 stitches plus 1.

1. Row 1 (RS): K1, *yo, ssk, k1; repeat from * to end.
2. Row 2 (WS): K1, *yo, p2tog, k1; repeat from * to end.
3. Repeat rows 1 and 2 for lace rib.

TRIANGLE LACE

This very textured lace pattern is great for baby blankets, throws, and scarves. You work this pattern over an odd number of stitches.

1. Row 1 (RS): K1, *yo, slip 1, k1, yo, pass the k st and the yo over; repeat from * to end.
2. Row 2 (WS): *P2, drop the yo from the previous row; repeat from * to last stitch, p1.
3. Row 3: K2, *yo, slip 1, k1, yo, pass the k st and the yo over; repeat from * to last stitch, k1.
4. Row 4: P3, *drop the yo from the previous row, p2; repeat from * to end.
5. Repeat rows 1–4 for triangle lace.

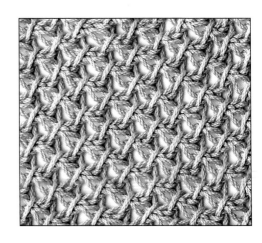

DIAGONAL LACE

This is a simple lace that is lovely for baby clothes and summer cardigans. This pattern uses the decrease slip, slip, knit, abbreviated ssk. You work this pattern on a multiple of 6 stitches.

① Row 1 (RS): *[K1, yo, ssk] twice; repeat from * to end.

② Rows 2, 4, and 6 (WS): Purl.

③ Row 3: *K2, yo, ssk, k2; repeat from * to end.

④ Row 5: *K3, yo, ssk, k1; repeat from * to end.

⑤ Repeat rows 1–6 for diagonal lace.

ARROWHEAD LACE

This lace pattern is easy to follow and works well worked on a shawl or throw. You work this pattern on a multiple of 6 stitches plus 1.

① Row 1 and all odd-numbered rows (WS): Purl.

② Row 2 (RS): K3, *yo, ssk, k4; repeat from * to last 4 stitches, yo, ssk, k2.

③ Row 4: K1, *K2tog, yo, k1, yo, ssk, k1; repeat from * to end.

④ Row 6: K2tog, yo, *K3, yo, slip 1, k2tog, psso, yo; repeat from * to last 5 stitches, k3, yo, ssk.

⑤ Rows 8 and 10: K1, *yo, ssk, k1, k2tog, yo, k1; repeat from * to end.

⑥ Repeat rows 1–10 for arrowhead lace.

LACE LEAF PANEL

This 9-stitch panel works well as an accent. Try it on throws or centered on sleeves.

① Row 1 (RS): P3, [k1, yo] twice, k1, p3.

② Rows 2 and 8 (WS): K3, p5, k3.

③ Row 3: P3, k2, yo, k1, yo, k2, p3.

④ Rows 4 and 6: K3, p7, k3.

⑤ Row 5: P3, ssk, k1, [yo, k1] twice, k2tog, p3.

⑥ Row 7: P3, ssk, k3, k2tog, p3.

⑦ Row 9: P3, ssk, k1, k2tog, p3.

⑧ Rows 10 and 12: K3, p3, k3.

⑨ Row 11: P3, yo, slip 2 tog knitwise, k1, pass the 2 slipped stitches tog over, yo, p3.

⑩ Repeat rows 1–12 for lace leaf panel.

chapter 10

Color Knitting

So far you have learned a lot about how to use knit and purl stitches to create patterns. In this chapter, it's time to think about using color to create beautiful, vibrant designs. There are several methods of using color in knitting: simple horizontal striping; Fair Isle knitting, which involves the stranding of two colors in one row; and intarsia knitting, which involves the use of bobbins to create isolated blocks of color.

One of the many joys of knitting is the planning stage: choosing colors that work well together—whether they be variations of the same blue hue or high-contrast opposites. If you choose colors that you love, either by themselves or in conjunction with other colors, you will enjoy your knitting even more.

Choosing Colors That Work Together

Sometimes it's hard to choose colors that go well together. You may find yourself drawn to the same color combinations over and over again and decide you need a nudge in a new direction; or perhaps the color combination you would choose is not available in a particular yarn. Looking at books on color knitting can help. Or you can use a color wheel like this one. To use it, you simply choose a starting color. Then you aim one of the points of the triangles or rectangles to the starting color and see what colors the color selector recommends. You may find a color combination that you never would have thought of on your own.

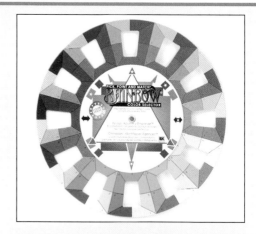

Here is a combination of three colors that was chosen using a color selector. Opposites often work well together, as long as they're not so bright that they vibrate and are hard to look at. Sets of opposites are blue and orange, red and green, and yellow and violet. The next time you're at a yarn shop, try comparing variations of these combinations to see how they work together.

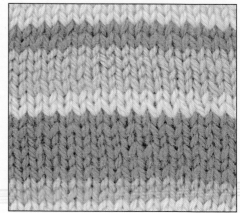

Experimenting with Color

When you're shopping for a knitting project, you will often find that you like the design or shaping of a garment but not the suggested color combination. On the other hand, you may see a color combination you love, but the sweater may not be one you like. You may also have to choose new colors out of necessity: The yarn shop may not stock the colors the pattern specifies, or those colors may be discontinued. In any case, it's a good idea to experiment with color arrangements first, so that you are sure your choice works. See how different the same design can look in varied colorways?

TIP

Tweeds and Variegated Yarns

Not every knitter is an expert on color, and some are downright scared of putting strong colors together in the same piece, for fear that their finished product will be loud or unattractive. For the color-wary, tweeds and variegated yarns can be a good entry into color knitting. Some tweeds are simply two colors of yarn plied together to form one yarn. Another type of tweed is made by spinning flecks of color onto a strand of a single color. Variegated yarns are produced by dying yarn in more than one color at varied intervals. The good thing about working with variegated yarn—especially for a beginner—is that you don't have to keep changing yarns to make your knitting colorful.

Make Horizontal Stripes

If you know how to knit and purl and how to change to a new ball of yarn (see page 28), you can knit horizontal stripes.

Stripe patterns are easiest to knit if you use an even number of rows for each stripe. This way, changing colors always occurs at the same edge, enabling you to carry the yarn up the side of your work, and ultimately saving you the trouble of weaving in a lot of ends later.

How to Make Horizontal Stripes in Stockinette

1 To make a stripe in a contrast color, work as many rows as you want the first stripe to be. At the beginning of the next row, drop the old yarn and knit or purl across the row in the new yarn, depending on which side you are on.

2 Carry the yarns up the side by twisting the first yarn around the second yarn at the edge of every other row. (If the stripes are only two rows each, this isn't necessary.)

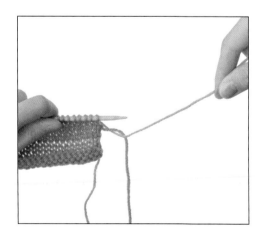

How to Make Horizontal Stripes in Ribbing

1 Using the desired ribbing pattern, work as many rows as you want the first stripe to be, ending with a wrong side row.

2 At the beginning of the next row, drop the old yarn and knit all stitches in the new color. (If you work this color change row in the ribbing pattern, the color break will not look tidy.)

This striped ribbing illustrates the result of working the color change row in the rib pattern. Little nubs of the old color appear along the color break, producing an uneven line.

FAQ

I am making a striped hat in the round. Every time I change colors, I get a little stair step of color at the beginning of the round, so the striping is not seamless. Is there anything I can do about this?

Yes. Here's what you do to significantly reduce the stair step effect:

1. When you're about to begin the round in the new color, pick up the stitch in the round below and put it onto the left needle.

2. Knit the first stitch in the new color and the picked-up stitch together as one. The picked up stitch conceals the uneven step.

3. Repeat steps 1 and 2 at each color change.

Learn Fair Isle Knitting

Fair Isle knitting is a method of knitting that probably originated in Fair Isle, one of the smallest of the Shetland Islands, off northern Scotland. It involves working with two colors across a row, carrying both yarns across the back. The challenge in Fair Isle knitting is maintaining tension: If the yarns stranded along the back are too tight, your knitting will pucker and have no elasticity; if they are too loose, your stitches will look uneven.

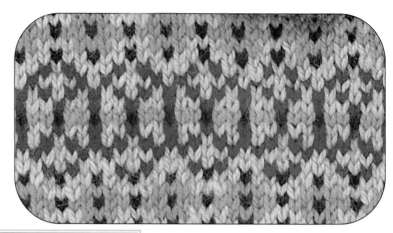

One-Handed Stranding versus Two-Handed Stranding

There are several ways to approach color knitting. When the intervals between color changes are no more than 4 stitches, you can do one-handed or two-handed stranding. *One-handed stranding* involves knitting in your usual way but alternating colors according to the pattern. *Two-handed stranding*, which is more efficient and results in an effortlessly neater back, requires holding one color in each hand, working the English method and the Continental method at the same time to alternate colors without stopping. With either type of stranding, when you work more than 4 stitches successively of one color, you have to weave or twist the color not in use in and out of the backs of those stitches.

ONE-HANDED STRANDING: KNIT SIDE

To avoid puckering, you need to keep the stitches on the right needle spread apart so you can strand a sufficient length of the non-working yarn across the back.

1 Work to the point in the row where you need to change colors. Let go of yarn A, pick up yarn B and bring it above and over yarn A, and knit the correct number of stitches in yarn B.

2 Work to the point in the row where you need to change colors again. Let go of yarn B, pick up yarn A and bring it underneath yarn B, and knit until the next color shift.

3 Repeat steps 1 and 2, taking care to keep yarn A underneath yarn B when changing colors.

> **Note:** *Always carry both yarns to the end of the row because the color pattern may call for the other color to begin the next row.*

ONE-HANDED STRANDING: PURL SIDE

1 Work to the point in the row where you need to change colors. Let go of yarn A, pick up yarn B and bring it above and over yarn A, and purl the correct number of stitches in yarn B.

2 When you reach the point in the row where you need to change colors again, let go of yarn B, pick up yarn A and bring it underneath yarn B, and purl until the next color shift.

3 Repeat steps 1 and 2, taking care to keep yarn A underneath yarn B when changing colors.

Note: Always carry both yarns to the end of the row because the color pattern may call for the other color to begin the next row.

CONTINUED ON NEXT PAGE

FAQ

How can I keep my yarns from getting tangled when I'm color knitting?

It helps to consistently keep the same yarn above and the same yarn below when changing colors. Also, you should take care not to twist yarns when you turn your knitting to switch from the right side to the wrong side and vice versa. Some knitters keep each ball of yarn in its own plastic container or small box to keep the yarns from rolling around and getting tangled. That way, if the yarns do get tangled, it's easy to just move the containers around to correct the problem.

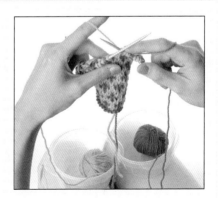

TWO-HANDED STRANDING: KNIT SIDE

Two-handed stranding is an excellent way to work Fair Isle knitting. If you want to simply practice knitting with both hands at the same time, you should try a very easy two-color pattern first so that you can focus on technique.

① Hold yarn A in your right hand, English style, and yarn B in your left hand, Continental style.

② Knit with yarn A in your right hand, holding it above yarn B, to the point in the row where you need to change colors.

③ Knit with your left hand using yarn B, which should automatically come from underneath yarn A.

④ Repeat steps 1–3 across the row.

Note: *Always carry both yarns to the end of the row because the color pattern may call for the other color to begin the next row.*

TWO-HANDED STRANDING: PURL SIDE

1 Hold yarn A in your right hand, English style, and yarn B in your left hand, Continental style.

2 Purl with yarn A in your right hand, holding it above yarn B, to the point in the row where you need to change colors.

3 Purl with your left hand using yarn B, which should automatically come from underneath yarn A.

4 Repeat steps 1–3 across the row.

Note: *Always carry both yarns to the end of the row because the color pattern may call for the other color to begin the next row.*

FAQ

When I knit Fair Isle patterns, my knitting doesn't pucker, but I don't get the same gauge as I do with stockinette stitch using the same yarn on the same size needles. I want to make a sweater that combines both techniques, but I'm worried that the gauge will not be uniform. Is there something I can do to compensate?

Fair Isle knitting can affect gauge. Usually, the row gauge is closer to or equal to the stitch gauge because Fair Isle stitches have a more square appearance. It is not uncommon for the stitch gauge to be slightly compressed. If you're working on a fabric that combines large blocks of non–Fair Isle with segments of Fair Isle, you might try working the Fair Isle section in needles one size larger. You can try working up a gauge sample that combines the stitches used to see if this works for you.

Weave Yarns in Color Knitting

When you're working with a color pattern in which there are more than 4 stitches between color changes or more than two colors per row, you need to carry the non-working yarn along the back by weaving it in and out of the backs of every few stitches made in the working yarn. How you do this depends on whether you're knitting or purling, as well as on which hand is holding the working yarn and which is holding the weaving yarn.

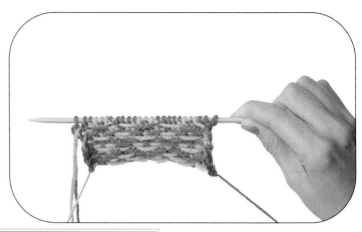

Weaving In, Knit Side: Working Yarn Right, Weaving Yarn Left

You should hold yarn A, the working yarn, in your right hand, English style, and yarn B, the yarn that will be woven in back, in your left hand, Continental style.

1. Insert the right needle into the next stitch on the left needle. Move your finger to bring yarn B from back to front and lay it against the tip of the right needle. Wrap yarn A as usual to prepare to knit the stitch.

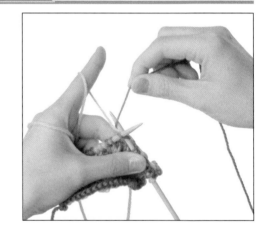

2. Knit the stitch.

3. Move your finger to bring yarn B away from the needles as usual. When you knit the next stitch, yarn B gets caught under the horizontal bar between this new stitch and the last stitch.

Weaving In, Knit Side: Working Yarn Left, Weaving Yarn Right

You should hold yarn A, the weaving yarn, in your right hand, English style, and yarn B, the working yarn, in your left hand, Continental style.

1 Insert the right needle into the next stitch on the left needle. Wrap yarn A around the right needle as you would to knit; then wrap yarn B around the right needle as you would to knit.

2 Bring yarn A back off the right needle to where it came from, leaving yarn B wrapped around the right needle, ready to be knit.

3 Knit the stitch.

CONTINUED ON NEXT PAGE

Weaving In, Purl Side: Working Yarn Right, Weaving Yarn Left

You should hold yarn A, the working yarn, in your right hand, English style, and yarn B, the yarn that will be woven in back, in your left hand, Continental style.

1 Insert the right needle into the next stitch as if to purl. Move your finger to bring yarn B from front to back and lay it against the tip of the right needle. Wrap yarn A as usual to prepare to purl the stitch.

2 Purl the stitch.

3 Before purling the next stitch, bring yarn B down and away from the needles as shown (a); wrap yarn A as usual and then purl the stitch (b).

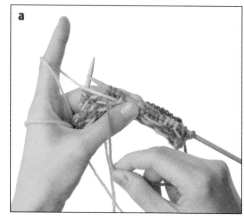

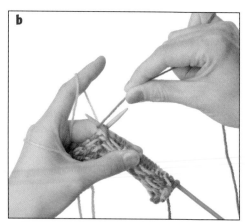

Weaving In, Purl Side: Working Yarn Left, Weaving Yarn Right

You should hold yarn A, the weaving yarn, in your right hand, English style, and yarn B, the working yarn, in your left hand, Continental style.

1 Insert the right needle into the next stitch as if to purl. Bring yarn A under the right needle from front to back; then lay yarn B over the tip of the right needle from front to back.

2 Bring yarn A back to the front—to where it came from (it will be hooked around yarn B)—and then draw yarn B through to purl the stitch.

3 Hold yarn A down away from the needles and purl another stitch using yarn B.

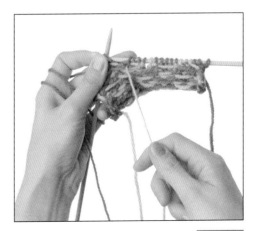

Experiment with a Few Simple Color Patterns

Here are a few simple color knitting patterns that you can try. Most of them employ only two colors so that you can get a feel for Fair Isle without getting overwhelmed by using too many yarn ends and color symbols. Each pattern is illustrated with a stitch pattern chart and a companion color key. See page 86 for information on reading charts.

Color Patterns

COLOR PATTERN 1: TWO COLORS

This 6-stitch repeat can be used as a border when worked over just four rows, or it can be used as a stripe pattern if repeated every six rows.

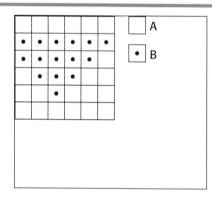

A

• B

Color chart

COLOR PATTERN 2: TWO COLORS

This 6-stitch, four-row repeat is an easy allover pattern.

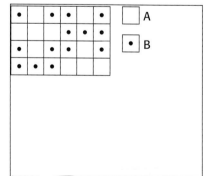

A

• B

Color chart

COLOR PATTERN 3: TWO COLORS

This 8-stitch border pattern works well at the hem or cuff of a Fair Isle sweater.

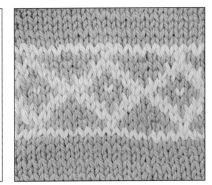

Color chart

COLOR PATTERN 4: THREE COLORS

This 4-stitch repeat looks great worked over seven rows along a border.

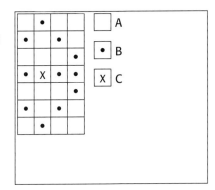

Color chart

COLOR PATTERN 5: TWO COLORS

This 4-stitch, 12-row repeat creates a very modern-looking allover pattern.

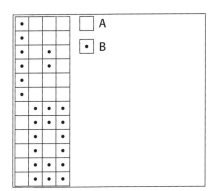

Color chart

Try Intarsia

Intarsia, or *bobbin knitting*, is a form of color knitting. Unlike Fair Isle—where colors are worked and carried across rows in a repetitive pattern—with intarsia you can scatter isolated blocks of color over your knitting or put one large motif on a background of another color. You knit each motif using a separate ball(s) or bobbin(s) of yarn. When changing colors, you twist yarns together on the wrong side to avoid having holes on the right side.

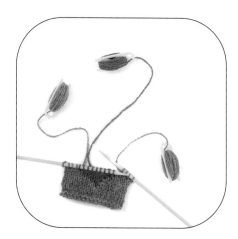

Intarsia with Two Colors

Before beginning an intarsia project, you should wind your main and contrast colors onto two or three bobbins for each color.

1 On the right side, knit to the place where the intarsia motif is to begin, drop the main color yarn, and get ready to knit with the contrast color yarn.

Note: *You might want to tie the new yarn to the old yarn before knitting the first stitch of the new color. This helps maintain even tension. You can untie it and secure the loose end later. Just be sure to leave at least a 6-inch tail on the new yarn.*

2 Knit as many stitches in the contrast color as your pattern calls for.

3 Drop the contrast color and begin knitting from a new bobbin of your main color. Work to the end of the right side row.

Note: *When changing colors on the right side, pick up the new yarn from underneath the old yarn to twist the yarns together on the back. This prevents gaps where the two colors meet.*

4 On the wrong side, purl using the main color until you reach the point where the color change should occur.

5 Drop the main color, twist the yarns together by bringing the contrast color up from underneath the main color, and purl as many stitches in the contrast color as the pattern requires.

6 Drop the contrast color, twist the yarns together by picking up the main color from underneath the contrast color, and purl the next stitch. Continue as the pattern directs.

Here are a few simple intarsia motifs that you can practice on or incorporate into your knitting. Before you begin, be sure to wind bobbins in the main color as well as the contrast colors for the motif.

Intarsia Motifs

INTARSIA HEART

This is an easy motif that adds a warm, homey touch to just about any knitted piece.

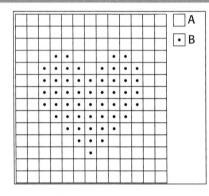

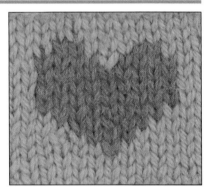

Color chart

INTARSIA STAR

This star adds a fun accent to a rolled-brim hat or centered on the front of a pullover.

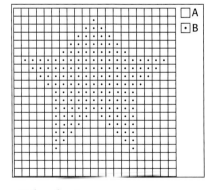

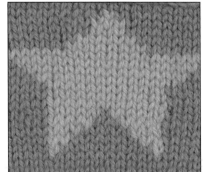

Color chart

INTARSIA DUCK

This is a perfect motif for baby sweaters and blankets.

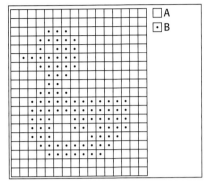

Color chart

INTARSIA BUTTERFLY

This motif can be embellished with embroidery (see pages 188–189) for added color.

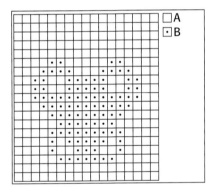

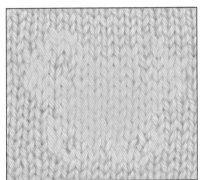

Color chart

INTARSIA FLOWER

This motif uses two contrast colors. Like the star, it adds a whimsical accent to a hat or sweater.

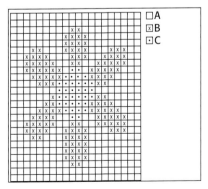

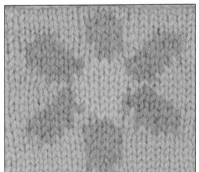

Color chart

chapter 11

Finishing Techniques

When you complete the knitting stage of a project, it's time to move on to finishing. *Finishing* involves weaving in all the loose ends hanging off your knitting, blocking your pieces to the correct measurements, and putting the project together by sewing seams. Although most knitters prefer knitting to finishing, mastering tidy finishing techniques will ensure that you are happy with your completed projects.

Weave In Ends

Weaving in ends is what you do to get rid of all the loose yarns dangling from your knitting. The instructions so far have said to leave ends no shorter than 6 inches. You need at least that length to properly weave in an end.

To weave in ends, you need a pair of scissors and a tapestry needle that is appropriate for the thickness of yarn you are using. You can weave in ends either horizontally across the work or vertically up the side of the work.

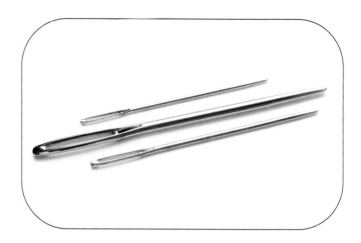

How to Weave In Ends up the Side

① With the wrong side facing, thread a tail of yarn through a tapestry needle.

② Bring the tapestry needle in and out from back to front up the side of the knitting.

③ After you have woven in the end a few inches, cut it close to the work, taking great care not to cut your knitting.

How to Weave In Ends Horizontally Across Stitches

1 With the wrong side facing, thread the tail of yarn through the tapestry needle.

2 Weave the tapestry needle in and out of the backs of the stitches in a straight diagonal line for 2 to 3 inches.

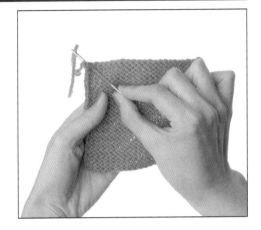

3 Weave the tapestry needle in and out of the backs of the stitches in the opposite direction, right next to the first diagonal line, for about 1 inch.

4 Cut the yarn end close to the work, taking great care not to cut your knitting.

Note: You can lightly stretch your knitting to pull the yarn end further into the work to conceal it.

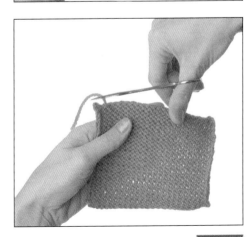

Block Your Knitting

Blocking is a wonderful fixer of imperfections. It involves moistening knitted pieces, shaping them, and allowing them to dry so that they hold the proper shape, to the correct measurements.

To block a project, you need a padded surface that is big enough to lay your largest piece of knitting flat, a set of long, rustproof pins, and a measuring tape. For wet blocking, you need a clean spray bottle; for steam blocking, you need a steam iron or hand steamer.

Wet Blocking

Wet blocking involves wetting your knitted pieces thoroughly, without using a steam iron. You can wet the pieces by immersing them in a basin of water or, even easier, you can pin them to their proper measurements beforehand and wet them with a spray bottle. Before wet blocking, be sure to read your ball band to ensure that washing in water is safe for your yarn. Wet blocking is best for wool blends, some synthetics, and hairy yarns like angora and mohair. It works wonders on textured and cable knits.

① Lay a knitted piece flat on a padded surface. Pin only at enough points to hold the piece straight for the time being.

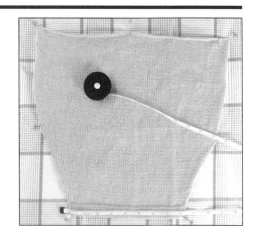

② Measure the knitted piece to ensure that it has the same dimensions that the pattern specifies. Adjust the pins, as necessary, to match the measurements and to make the piece even.

Note: Do not stretch and pin ribbing at cuffs and hems unless the pattern indicates to do so. After ribbing is stretched and blocked, it is no longer elastic.

③ When the measurements are correct, pin the piece all around.

④ Wet the piece thoroughly with a spray bottle.

⑤ Allow the piece to dry and then remove the pins.

Repeat steps 1–5 for all pieces of your project. Be sure that all the pieces are completely dry before sewing the seams.

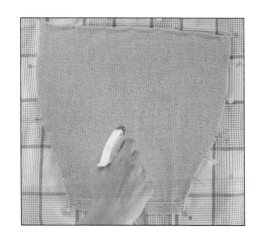

Steam Blocking

Steam blocking involves using a steam iron or hand steamer. You can get fast results with steam blocking because the drying time is shorter than with wet blocking. Again, you need to check your ball band's care instructions to ensure that it is safe to apply steam to your yarn and at what temperature. Steam blocking is best for wool, cotton, cashmere, and alpaca. The key to steam blocking is not to press the knitting with the iron, but to run the iron lightly above the knitting to steam it. Lay a light cloth, such as a pillowcase, over the piece to be blocked; this will protect your work from the high heat and any potential staining.

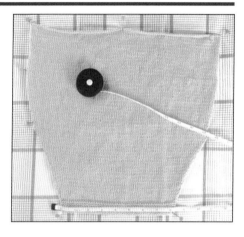

1 Lay a knitted piece flat on a padded surface. Pin only at enough points to hold the piece straight for the time being.

2 Measure the knitted piece to ensure that it has the same dimensions that the pattern specifies. Adjust the pins as necessary to match the measurements and to make the piece even.

Note: Do not stretch and pin ribbing at cuffs and hems unless the pattern indicates to do so. After ribbing is stretched and blocked, it is no longer elastic.

3 When the measurements are correct, pin the piece all around.

4 Cover the piece with a light cloth. (You can dampen the cloth with a spray bottle, if desired.) Slowly and gently, run the iron over the entire piece, excluding ribbing, taking care not to press or distort the knitting.

5 Allow the piece to dry and then remove the pins.

6 Repeat steps 1–5 for all pieces of your project. Be sure that all the pieces are completely dry before sewing the seams.

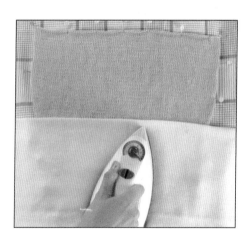

Sew Seams

There are numerous ways to sew seams. Some seams are best for shoulders, while others are preferable for vertical seams or certain stitch patterns. Taking time and care when sewing blocked pieces together is well worth the effort.

You should sew seams with a tapestry needle and the main color yarn used to knit the project. When knitting with novelty yarns, you should sew seams with a matching plied yarn that calls for the same care instructions as the main yarn.

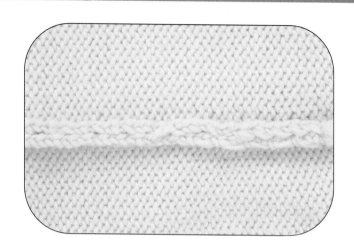

Invisible Horizontal Seam

This seam is an excellent choice for bound-off shoulder seams. It is used to join a horizontal edge to another horizontal edge. When it is done correctly, the join appears seamless.

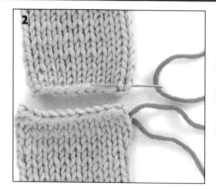

1. Thread a tapestry needle with a long enough strand of yarn to sew the seam and leave a 6-inch tail.

2. With right sides up, line up the bound-off edges exactly. Insert the needle from back to front through the middle of the first stitch of the lower piece, leaving a 6-inch tail.

3. Use the needle to pick up the two loops (the V) of the corresponding stitch on the upper piece. Pull the yarn through.

4. Bring the needle across the seam to the next stitch on the lower piece and use it to pick up the loops (the upside-down V), threading it through all the way.

5. Repeat steps 3 and 4 across the seam, pulling the yarn lightly—but not too tightly, or it will pucker—every couple stitches to neaten it.

6. Weave in the loose ends.

   Note: A contrast color yarn was used here to sew the seam for illustrative purposes. Be sure to sew your seams with the yarn used to knit the pieces for your seams.

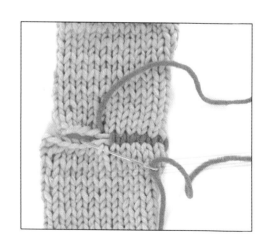

Backstitch Seam

You can use this firm seam almost anywhere in constructing a project. You work it with the right sides of the pieces facing each other, so that they are inside out. You should work it about 1 stitch in from the edge.

1 Thread a tapestry needle with a long enough strand of yarn to sew the seam and leave a 6-inch tail.

2 Place the pieces together, with the right sides facing each other and the seam edge lined up. Secure the edge stitches by bringing the needle through both thicknesses from back to front at the right edge, 1 stitch down from the bound-off stitches. Do this twice and pull the yarn through.

3 Insert the needle through both thicknesses, from back to front, about 2 stitches to the left, and bring the yarn through.

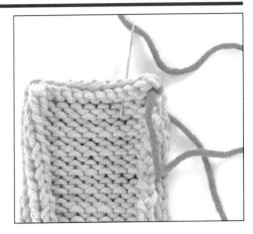

4 Insert the needle from front to back, about 1 stitch in to the right, and pull the yarn through.

5 Now bring the needle ahead 2 stitches to the left and insert it from back to front.

6 Repeat steps 4 and 5 across the seam until you reach the end, taking care to insert the needle at the same depth each time.

7 Weave in the loose ends.

Note: A contrast color yarn was used here to sew the seam for illustrative purposes. Be sure to sew your seams with the yarn used to knit the pieces for your seams.

CONTINUED ON NEXT PAGE

Invisible Vertical Seam

This seam works beautifully for sweater sides and underarm seams. It lays flat and is invisible.

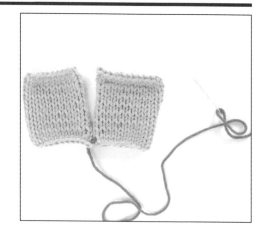

1. Thread a tapestry needle with a long enough strand of yarn to sew your seam and leave a 6-inch tail.

2. With the right sides up, line up the vertical edges exactly. Sew 1 stitch at the base of the seam to join the pieces: Insert the needle from back to front through the space between the first and second stitches on the lower-right corner of the left piece, pulling yarn through until only about 6 inches remains; insert the needle from front to back between the first and second stitches in the lower-left corner of the right piece; bring the needle back through the same spot on the left piece again. Pull the yarn through snugly.

   Now you are ready to work the invisible vertical seam.

3. Find the horizontal bar of yarn between the first and second stitches. Insert the needle under that horizontal bar, between the first and second stitches, 1 stitch up from the joining stitch, on the right piece. Pull the yarn through.

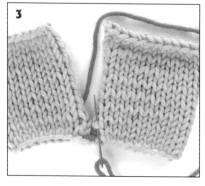

4. Insert the needle under the horizontal bar between the first and second stitches, 1 stitch up from the joining stitch, on the left piece. Pull the yarn through.

5. Insert the needle under the next horizontal bar up on the right side and then under the corresponding bar on the left side. Continue in this manner, alternating from side to side, to the end of the seam.

6. Weave in the loose ends.

   Note: *A contrast color yarn was used here to sew the seam for illustrative purposes. Be sure to sew your seams with the yarn used to knit the pieces for your seams.*

Invisible Vertical-to-Horizontal Seam

This seam is excellent for joining a bound-off edge to a side edge, as in joining a sleeve cap to an armhole.

1. Thread a tapestry needle with a long enough strand of yarn to sew your seam and leave a 6-inch tail.

2. With the right sides facing, line up the bound-off edge and the side edge.

3. Insert the needle from back to front through the V of the first stitch on the right side of the lower piece, below the bound-off edge, and pull the yarn through until about 6 inches remain.

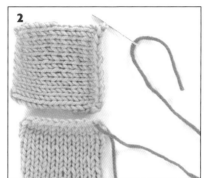
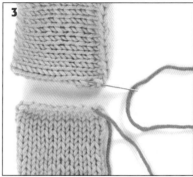

4. Insert the needle on the other side of the join—directly across from the same point on the vertical piece—under one of the bars between the first and second stitches on the horizontal piece. Pull the yarn through.

Note: Because you are matching rows to stitches in this join, and because there are usually more rows per inch than stitches, you need to pick up two of the bars on the horizontal piece every other stitch or so to keep the seam even.

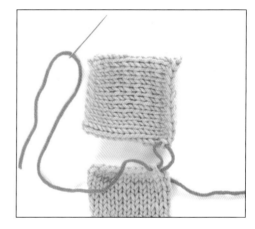

5. Bring the yarn across the join and pick up the loops that make the point of the upside-down V of the next stitch on the vertical piece, pulling the yarn through, trying to imitate the size of each stitch in the knitted piece.

6. Continue alternating back and forth between the upper and lower pieces until you finish the seam.

7. Weave in the loose ends.

Note: A contrast color yarn was used here to sew the seam for illustrative purposes. Be sure to sew your seams with the yarn used to knit the pieces for your seams.

Grafting—which is a good choice for unshaped shoulders, toes of socks, and mitten tips—involves joining an open row of stitches to another open row of stitches or to another edge. The stitches are joined while they're still on the knitting needle, and the final result looks like a row of stockinette stitch. The two grafting methods covered here are Kitchener stitch and the three-needle bind-off.

Kitchener Stitch

To prepare to join edges with Kitchener stitch, put each set of stitches onto a knitting needle.

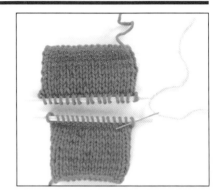

1 Using yarn that matches your knitting, thread a tapestry needle with a strand that is roughly twice the length of the seam.

2 Lay both pieces of knitting on a table, with the wrong sides down and the needles running parallel to each other, with the tips facing to the right.

3 Insert the tapestry needle into the first stitch on the lower needle as if to purl; pull the yarn through until only about 6 inches remain. Leave the stitch on the needle.

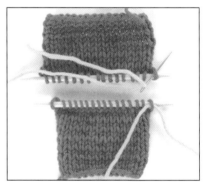

4 Insert the tapestry needle into the first stitch on the upper needle as if to knit and pull the yarn through snugly, leaving the stitch on the needle.

5 Insert the tapestry needle into the first stitch on the lower needle again, this time as if to knit (a); then slip this stitch off the needle (b).

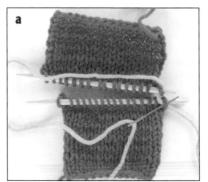

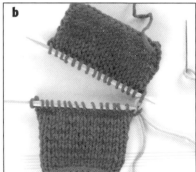

6 Insert the tapestry needle into the next stitch on the lower needle as if to purl. Leave the stitch on the needle.

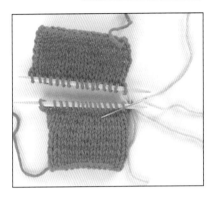

7 Insert the tapestry needle into the first stitch on the upper needle again, this time as if to purl (a); then slip this stitch off the needle (b).

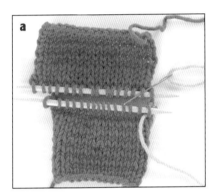
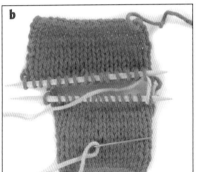

8 Insert the tapestry needle into the next stitch on the upper needle as if to knit. Leave the stitch on the needle.

9 Repeat steps 5–8 until all the stitches have been completed. Remember: On the lower needle, the first insertion is as if to purl, the second insertion is as if to knit, and then the stitch comes off; on the upper needle, the first insertion is as if to knit, the second insertion is as if to purl, and then the stitch comes off.

Note: A contrast color yarn was used here to sew the seam for illustrative purposes. Be sure to sew your seams with the yarn used to knit the pieces for your seams.

CONTINUED ON NEXT PAGE

Three-Needle Bind-Off

You can use this method to join a seam by knitting and binding off the two sets of stitches together. To prepare to join edges with the three-needle bind-off, you need to put each set of stitches onto a knitting needle and have handy a third knitting needle. If one of the sets of stitches has the working yarn still attached, you can use that to knit the seam; otherwise, you can use a piece of the same yarn you used to knit the pieces.

① Hold the needles parallel, with the right sides of your knitting facing each other, as shown.

② Insert a third knitting needle into the first stitch on the front needle as if to knit and then into the first stitch on the back needle as if to knit. Wrap the working yarn around the tip of the third needle as you would to knit normally.

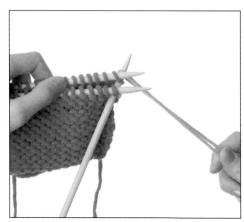

③ Bring the loop through the first stitch on the back needle, just as you would to knit, and then bring the same loop all the way through to the front of the first stitch on the front needle as well.

④ Slip both old stitches off the parallel needles, just as you would to knit them. You should now have 1 stitch on the third needle.

⑤ Repeat steps 2–4 a second time. There should now be 2 stitches on the right needle.

⑥ Pass the first stitch on the right needle over the second to bind off.

⑦ Continue knitting together the corresponding stitches from each needle and binding off as you go, until only 1 stitch remains on the right needle. Cut the yarn, leaving a 6-inch tail, and pull the tail through the last stitch to secure.

⑧ Weave in the loose ends.

Note: A contrast color yarn was used here to sew the seam for illustrative purposes. Be sure to sew your seams with the yarn used to knit the pieces for your seams.

How to Assemble a Sweater

Now that you are familiar with several different ways to attach knit pieces to each other, you can assemble a simple sweater. How a sweater is made—whether it is knit in the round or on straight needles, how the sleeves are created, whether it is a cardigan or a pullover—determines not only how it is put together but also the order in which the pieces are assembled.

ORDER OF ASSEMBLY

Generally, sweaters that are knit flat in pieces are joined first at the shoulders. Then the sleeves are attached. Finally, the side and underarm seams are sewn. You use long straight pins to pin pieces together before seaming. You should neaten up seams by lightly steaming with an iron as you go.

WHICH SEAM TECHNIQUE FOR WHICH PART?

Sometimes knitting instructions specify the best seaming technique for a given join. If no specific technique is indicated, you can always safely use the backstitch seam for the shoulders, whether they are shaped or not. If the shoulders are not shaped, you can try using the invisible horizontal seam or the three-needle bind-off. The invisible vertical seam is an excellent choice for side and underarm seams; but again, a backstitch seam is perfectly acceptable for those joins.

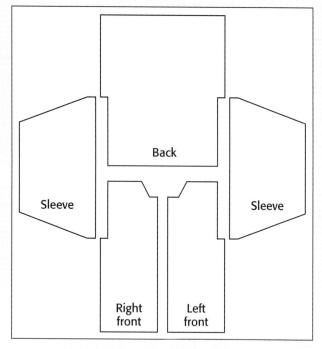

Type of Seam	Use It to Join	Examples
Invisible horizontal seam	Two horizontal edges	Bound-off shoulder seams
Backstitch seam	All edges	Shaped shoulders, side seams, add-on collars
Invisible vertical seam	Two vertical edges	Sweater sides and underarm seams
Invisible vertical-to-horizontal seam	A bound-off edge to a side edge	Joining a sleeve cap to an armhole
Grafted seam	Two horizontal edges	Unshaped shoulders, toes of socks, mitten tips

ATTACHING SLEEVES

There are many different ways to shape armholes and sleeve caps. The type of armhole shaping always determines the sleeve cap shaping. After blocking all pieces, working the edging on the neck, and joining and pressing shoulder seams, you can attach the sleeves. You need to find the center of the sleeve cap by folding the sleeve in half lengthwise, and then you mark the center with a pin. After pinning the center of the sleeve cap to the shoulder seam, with the right sides facing each other, you can pin the rest of the sleeve cap to the armhole, lining up the sleeve cap shaping with the corresponding armhole shaping. Then you can sew the sleeve in place by using a backstitch seam.

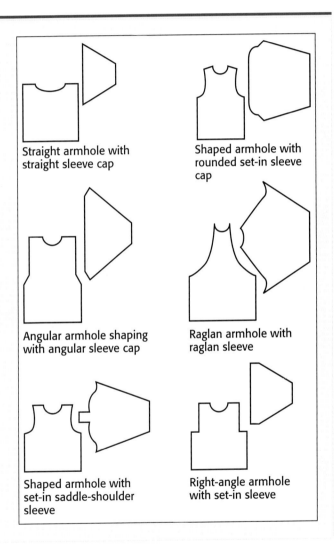

Straight armhole with straight sleeve cap

Shaped armhole with rounded set-in sleeve cap

Angular armhole shaping with angular sleeve cap

Raglan armhole with raglan sleeve

Shaped armhole with set-in saddle-shoulder sleeve

Right-angle armhole with set-in sleeve

chapter 12

Finishing Details

Sometimes the finishing phase of a hand-knit sweater can take almost as long as the knitting phase. Besides blocking and seaming pieces together, there are also many finishing details that may be called for, such as button bands, collars, hems, and pockets.

Picking up stitches is what you do to add button bands, neckbands, collars, or decorative borders to the already finished edges of your knitting. After you pick up stitches along an edge, you use them to knit the part you want to add—without having to sew the piece on. You can also pick up stitches at an armhole edge and knit a sleeve from the top down. You can pick up stitches along straight edges, as for button bands, or along curved edges, as for collars.

How to Pick Up Stitches Along a Bound-off Edge

Using a needle a size or two smaller than your working needles, pick up stitches, working from right to left.

① Start at the top-right corner, with the right side facing, and insert the needle into the center of the V of the first stitch, just below the bound-off row.

② Wrap the working yarn around the needle as you would to knit, holding a 6-inch tail, as shown.

③ Bring the loop of the working yarn to the front, as you would to knit.

You have now picked up your first stitch.

④ Repeat steps 1–3 across the edge, working from right to left, for each stitch.

Note: *When you are done picking up stitches and are ready to begin knitting, be sure to switch back to your working needles.*

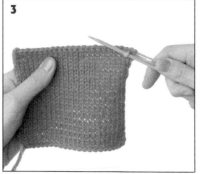

How to Pick Up Stitches Along a Vertical Edge

Picking up stitches along a vertical edge is very similar to picking them up along a bound-off edge, except that instead of inserting the needle into the center of each stitch along the horizontal row, you insert the needle into the spaces between the first and second stitches all along the vertical row.

1 Turn your work so that the vertical rows run horizontally and the right side is facing.

2 Starting at the right corner of the pick-up edge, insert the right needle from front to back into the space between the first and second stitches, as shown. Wrap the working yarn around the right needle as you would to knit, holding a 6-inch tail, as shown.

3 Bring the loop of working yarn to the front, as you would to knit.

You have now picked up your first stitch.

4 Repeat steps 1–3 across the edge, working from right to left, skipping a row every few stitches.

Note: Because there are more rows per inch than stitches, you do not need to insert the needle between every stitch along a vertical edge. Doing so results in an edge that looks stretched out; skipping a row every few pick-up stitches makes up for the difference.

CONTINUED ON NEXT PAGE

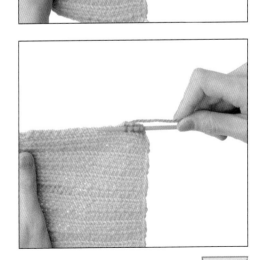

How to Pick Up Stitches Along a Curved Edge

You can combine what you know about picking up stitches along horizontal and bound-off edges when you pick up stitches along a curved edge, such as with neck shaping.

1 Starting at the top-right corner, with the right side facing, insert the needle into the center of the V of the first stitch, just below the bound-off edge of the shaping.

2 Wrap the working yarn around the needle, as you would to knit, holding a 6-inch tail, as shown.

3 Pick up all the stitches on the horizontal section of the shaping until you get to the vertical section.

4 Continue picking up stitches as you would for a vertical edge, skipping a row every few stitches, if necessary. Be sure not to insert the needle into any large holes caused by the shaping, as doing so will result in a hole in your picked-up edge.

How to Pick Up Stitches Evenly

Often, knitting instructions call for you to pick up a certain number of stitches evenly along an edge. If you don't think you can do this by eye, you can place markers at regular intervals along the edge to ensure that you pick up stitches evenly. If you don't pick up stitches evenly, your final result will look decidedly off: It will cinch in or look stretched.

1 Place pins, spaced evenly apart, along the edge where the stitches are to be picked up.

Note: Instead of using pins, you can tie bits of yarn as markers at even intervals along the edge.

2 Calculate how many stitches should be picked up between markers by dividing the total number of stitches to be picked up by the number of spaces between pins.

3 Pick up the appropriate number of stitches between each pair of markers.

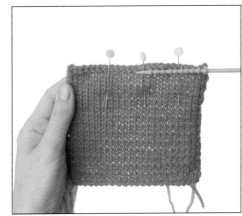

FAQ

My instructions call for picking up a large number of stitches continuously along the button bands and around the neck all at once. How can I fit so many stitches on the needle?

You should use a flexible circular needle to pick up and work stitches on long stretches. You will not be using the needle to knit in the round; instead, you'll use it to work back and forth, as you would with straight needles. If you're not sure what length to use, simply measure the length of the edge on which you need to pick up stitches and use the closest length of circular needle. Circular needles also work very well for collars and neckbands, so if your project calls for this type of treatment, be sure to equip yourself with the proper size of circular needle.

Some sweater patterns call for bands and collars that are knit as separate pieces and sewn on at the end. Others indicate that you knit the band or collar directly onto the garment by picking up stitches. Either way, it's a good idea to acquaint yourself with the various parts of a sweater.

BUTTON BANDS

Some cardigans are finished with strips of knitting along the vertical edge called *button bands*; one button band has buttonholes on it, and the other has buttons sewn to it. Button bands can be worked in various stitch patterns but are commonly worked in ribbing, seed stitch, or garter stitch, so they lie flat. They are frequently worked using needles that are one or two sizes smaller than the needles used for the garment, to give a neat appearance. When working button bands, you should knit the band that holds the buttons first; you mark the placement of the buttons on the band by using stitch markers, and then when you knit the buttonhole band, you work the buttonholes to correlate with your markings. You place buttons on the left band for women and on the right band for men.

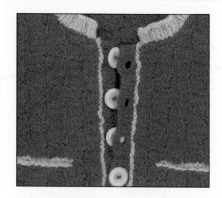

NECKBANDS

Like button bands, *neckbands* are frequently worked on smaller needles in ribbing, seed stitch, or garter stitch. Neck shaping by itself often has an unfinished or uneven look to it, so it is generally desirable to attach or knit on a neckband. There are many varieties of neckbands—crewneck, v-neck, and square neck, to name a few.

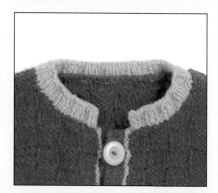

PLACKETS

Plackets are button bands that form an opening near the neck. Plackets can be placed vertically at the neck in either the front or back of a sweater, or they can be worked horizontally across the shoulder in place of a shoulder seam. Pullovers for babies and toddlers frequently use the latter version of plackets. You should work the button band portion of the placket first, mark it for button placement, and then work the buttonhole portion of the placket, working the buttonholes to correlate to the markings.

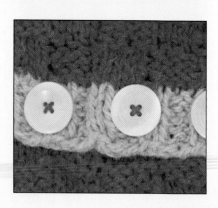

COLLARS

There are numerous *collar* styles to choose from. You work some collars by picking up the stitches around the neck and knitting on the collar directly; you work others as separate pieces that you sew on to the neck later.

When knitting a collar directly onto a sweater, you need to be sure to pick up stitches from the wrong side if the collar is going to fold down. One way to create a collar is to pick up stitches and work the collar in the round on double-pointed needles after joining the shoulders. Another method is to work back and forth with one shoulder still open and then sew a seam later.

You can work collars in a wide variety of stitch patterns; they can even have cables or color work involved. Most often, knitters want to use a stitch pattern that does not curl, such as ribbing, seed stitch, or garter stitch. When you make a collar in stockinette stitch, which does curl, it is a good idea to knit a flat-lying border around the edge of the collar to temper the curling.

Make Buttonholes

Different styles of sweaters call for different types of buttonholes. The size and type of button you're using also influences your choice of buttonhole. However, the eyelet buttonhole, the one-row horizontal buttonhole, and the two-row horizontal buttonhole should get you through most situations.

Before making buttonholes on your finished pieces, you should practice the various techniques a few times to make sure you come up with a nice, neat buttonhole.

How to Make a 1-Stitch Eyelet Buttonhole

This is the easiest buttonhole to make. It works very well for children's and babies' clothes, as well as for small buttons. It is worked by combining a yarn over with a knit 2 together: The yarn over makes the hole, and the knit 2 together decreases to maintain the original stitch count.

1 Work to the point where you want the buttonhole to be and then k2tog, yo; continue the row as established.

2 On the next row, work the yo as you would a regular stitch.

You have made a 1-stitch eyelet buttonhole.

How to Make a 2-Stitch Eyelet Buttonhole

This eyelet buttonhole is also easy, and it makes a larger hole than a 1-stitch eyelet buttonhole.

1 Work to the point where you want the buttonhole and then k2tog, yo twice, ssk; work the remainder of the row as previously established.

2 On the next row, work across until you get to the yarn overs. Purl into the first yo (a) and then purl into the back of the second yo (b); continue across the row as previously established.

You have made a 2-stitch eyelet buttonhole.

CONTINUED ON NEXT PAGE

How to Make a One-Row Horizontal Buttonhole

There are several methods for making horizontal buttonholes over two rows, but this one-row buttonhole looks much neater and does not need to be reinforced later.

1 On the right side, work to the point where you want the buttonhole to be placed. Bring the yarn to the front, slip the next stitch from the left needle as if to purl, and bring the yarn to the back. *Slip the next stitch from the left needle to the right and pass the first slipped stitch over it and off the needle. Repeat from * three times, keeping the yarn at the back the whole time.

You have bound off 4 stitches.

2 Slip the last bound-off stitch back to the left needle.

3 Turn your work so that the wrong side is facing and bring the yarn to the back.

4 Insert the right needle between the first and second stitches on the left needle and wrap the yarn around the right needle as if to knit.

5 Bring the loop through to the front as if to knit, but instead of slipping the old stitch off the left needle, use the right needle to place the new loop onto the left needle.

You have used the cable cast-on method to cast on 1 stitch.

6 Repeat steps 4 and 5 four more times and then turn the work back so that the RS is facing.

You have cast on 5 stitches.

7 Bring the yarn to the back and slip the first stitch from the left needle to the right needle; pass the additional cast-on stitch over the slipped stitch to close the buttonhole. Work to the end of the row as usual.

You have made a one-row horizontal buttonhole.

CONTINUED ON NEXT PAGE

How to Make a Two-Row Horizontal Buttonhole

This buttonhole is achieved by binding off stitches on one row and then casting on stitches on the next.

1 On the right side, work to the point where you want the buttonhole to be placed and then k2.

2 Insert the left needle from front to back into the first stitch of the pair just knit; then pull it over the second stitch and off the right needle (to bind off).

3 K1 and bring the stitch before it over and off the right needle.

4 Repeat step 3 two more times.

You have bound off 4 stitches for a buttonhole.

5 Work to the end of the row as usual.

6 On the wrong side, work until you get to the bound-off stitches.

7 Make a loop with the working yarn as shown; insert the right needle into the loop and pull to tighten.

You have used the simple cast-on method to cast on 1 stitch.

8 Repeat step 7 three more times.

You have cast on 4 stitches.

9 Work to the end of the row as usual.

You have completed a two-row horizontal buttonhole.

FAQ

I have a very large button. How can I make my buttonhole wide enough for such a large button?

You can make a horizontal buttonhole as wide as you like by using the two-row horizontal buttonhole method: You simply bind off as many stitches as will suit the size of your button and then cast on the same number of stitches on the following row.

Some buttonholes need to be reinforced so that they don't stretch out and become distorted. Reinforcing a buttonhole also gives it a tidy appearance. The two methods covered here—overcasting and buttonhole stitch—should suit any instance.

How to Reinforce Buttonholes by Overcasting

The overcasting method of finishing works well on eyelet buttonholes.

1 Thread a tapestry needle with matching or contrast color yarn.

2 Bring the tapestry needle through from back to front, leaving a 6-inch tail at the back, and loop the yarn from front to back around the perimeter of the buttonhole, as shown.

3 End your stitching on the wrong side. Cut the yarn, leaving a 6-inch tail.

4 Weave in the loose ends.

How to Finish Buttonholes by Using the Buttonhole Stitch

1 Thread a tapestry needle with matching or contrast color yarn.

2 Bring the tapestry needle through from back to front, leaving a 6-inch tail at the back.

3 Working from right to left, insert the tapestry needle from front to back, with the tip of the needle pointing toward the buttonhole, looping the yarn under the needle, as shown.

4 End your stitching on the wrong side. Cut the yarn, leaving a 6-inch tail.

5 Secure yarn ends at the back and weave in the loose ends.

Buttons and Other Fastenings

Another step in finishing many projects is choosing the right buttons, sewing in a zipper, or attaching some other form of fastener, such as snaps or clasps. Usually, a pattern specifies the dimensions of the buttons needed or the zipper length.

BUTTONS

Choosing buttons can be overwhelming because there are many styles and colors. You can immediately narrow down your choice based on size, but what style should you use for a particular project? If the work is very fine—small stitches or delicate openwork, for example—you might want to choose small and elegant buttons made of pearlized plastic or shell. For casual sweaters knit in tweeds or hand-spuns, wood or leather buttons can add the right touch. There are a lot of playful buttons—animals, faces, flowers, and insects—that work well on children's knits. Be sure to bring your project with you when choosing buttons. You will want to hold the buttons up to the knitting to see what looks best.

It's important to check for care instructions on a button's packaging. Some buttons are not washable and need to be removed before laundering. If you don't want to go to that trouble, be sure to choose washable buttons.

CLASPS

A lot of Norwegian sweaters call for pewter clasps instead of buttons. That doesn't mean you can't use them on a more contemporary design, as they do add a nice touch. Yarn shops that sell patterns for Scandinavian sweaters usually also sell clasps. You sew on clasps by using a needle and thread. You have to take care to place the two clasp components directly opposite each other so that the garment closes snugly.

ZIPPERS

Some cardigan and jacket patterns call for zippers. The pattern should indicate the zipper length and style—and perhaps even the color. After sewing together your garment, you pin the zipper in place and then sew it in by hand, using a needle and thread. You must be sure that the edge that the zipper is sewn to is the same length as the zipper, or your garment will be distorted. If sewing in a zipper is not something you feel comfortable with, but you really want to make the sweater, ask if your local yarn shop provides finishing services.

You can have fun with color by choosing a zipper that contrasts with your garment's main color. There are also numerous zipper pulls that can be added for accent. Or you can try tying to the zipper pull a pompom or tassel made in a matching or contrasting yarn.

Sewing a button onto your knitting is somewhat different from sewing a button onto a shirt because the knit fabric is a much looser weave. If your button's holes are large enough, you can use your knitting yarn to sew it in. Sometimes it's easier to separate your yarn into a few plies and use a thinner strand to sew the button.

How to Sew On a Button

1. Thread a tapestry needle as you would to sew your knitting, leaving a 6-inch tail coming out one side of the eye.

2. Insert the needle from back to front through the knitting and through one of the holes in the button. Pull the yarn through until you have about 6 inches of yarn left coming out the back of your knitting.

3. Insert the needle from front to back through another hole in your button and pull the yarn through all the way.

④ Continue until you have several stitches holding the button in place. With the yarn pulled through to the front of the fabric, but not through the button, wrap the yarn around the button stitches—between the back of the button and the front of the knitting—a few times. Then insert the needle back through the knitting to the wrong side.

⑤ Tie the two yarn ends in a knot and weave the ends into your knitting.

FAQ

My yarn is too thick to use to sew on my button. I would like to use thread, but the knot at the end keeps coming through the knitting. Is there something I can do to prevent this?

Yes. First, tie a knot in the end of your thread. Then insert the needle under the V where you want the button to be sewn and reinsert the needle between the strands near the knot. Pull it tight to secure the thread. Be sure to move the thread ends near the knot to the wrong side of your work and cut them short so they look tidy.

Knot

You can add a pocket to almost anything you knit—a sweater, a coat, a vest, or even a scarf. Patch pockets are the easiest to make. You just knit a square or rectangle to the size you want and sew it on to your knitting. Or you can pick up the stitches from your knitting and knit the patch pocket directly on. Inset pockets are a little more challenging, but if you know how to bind off, you can make those, too.

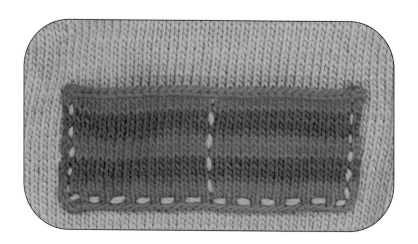

How to Attach a Patch Pocket

To attach a patch pocket, you need to first knit and steam block (see page 139) the pocket you want to sew on. (The sample here is a 4-inch square.) You also need a tapestry needle, straight pins, and yarn to sew the pocket.

1. Pin the pocket in place exactly where you want it to be. Thread a tapestry needle as you would to sew your knitting together, leaving a 6-inch tail coming out one side of the eye.

2. Insert the tapestry needle from back to front through both the knitting and the upper-right corner of the pocket. Loop the yarn around from front to back to front once more to reinforce the corner.

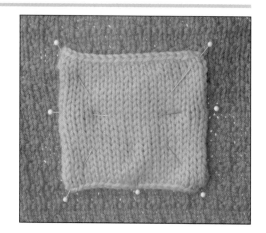

3. Sew on the pocket, using the overcast stitch you used to reinforce buttonholes on page 164, as shown, ending at the upper-left corner. Reinforce the corner as in step 2, ending with the needle on the wrong side.

4. Weave in the loose ends.

How to Pick Up a Patch Pocket

To pick up a patch pocket, you need straight pins, a tapestry needle, and yarn and needles to knit the pocket. You also need a knitting needle one or two sizes smaller than the one used to knit the garment; this is for picking up the pocket stitches.

1 Using straight pins, mark the outline of where you want the patch pocket to be on your garment.

2 Weave the smaller knitting needle under and over horizontally along the stitches where the base of the pocket will be.

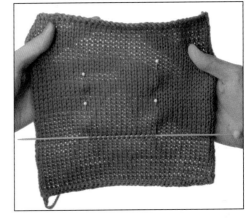

3 Using the yarn you intend to knit the pocket with and the working knitting needle, purl across the picked-up stitches. (This first row is a wrong side row.)

4 Beginning with a knit row, work from here in stockinette stitch (that is, knit across on the right side, purl across on the wrong side) until the pocket is the length you want it to be.

5 Bind off loosely.

6 Pin the pocket sides as shown.

7 Stitch the pockets sides in place, using the overcast stitch you used to reinforce buttonholes on page 164.

Note: *This stockinette stitch pocket has a rolled edge at the top. If you prefer a flat edge, try working the last ½ inch or so in ribbing, seed stitch, or garter stitch. You may also want to steam the pocket flap to neaten it up before sewing it in place.*

CONTINUED ON NEXT PAGE

How to Make an Inset Pocket

Inset pockets have a less noticeable appearance than patch pockets, as the front of the pocket is actually your knit garment. You knit the back of the pocket, or the lining, separately and put it on a stitch holder ahead of time; then you incorporate it when knitting the face of the garment that contains the pocket. You should follow your pattern's instructions for size and placement of an inset pocket. The following steps illustrate how to create an inset pocket.

① Knit the pocket lining(s) to the size indicated in your pattern's instructions. Instead of binding off the stitches, put them on a stitch holder. Steam the lining to block it (see page 139).

Note: Pocket linings are usually knit in stockinette stitch so that they lie flat. You can knit a pocket lining in the same color as the overall piece, or, if you prefer, you can knit the lining in an accent color.

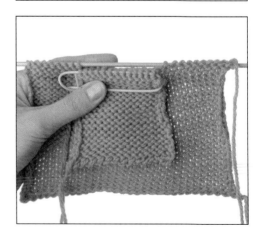

② On the piece of the garment that will hold the pocket (usually a cardigan front), work across the row on the right side to where the pocket will be placed. Bind off the same number of stitches as used to knit your pocket lining and work to the end of the row.

③ On the following row (wrong side), work across to the bound-off stitches. Hold your pocket lining so that the wrong side is facing you. (The right side of the lining should face the wrong side of the main garment piece.) Work across the lining stitches from the holder.

Note: You may have to slip your lining stitches from the holder to a needle if the stitch holder feels awkward or is not facing the right direction for you to work from it.

④ On the next row (right side), work across as usual.

⑤ Continue working this piece of the garment as established.

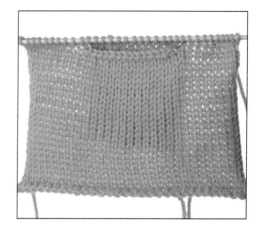

⑥ At the finishing stage of your garment, pin the bottom and sides of the pocket lining in place (a) and stitch to attach (b), using the overcast stitch you used to reinforce buttonholes on page 164.

⑦ Steam the sewn-in lining to flatten it, taking care not to press, which would bring the outline of the lining to the front of your work.

Note: *You can also make an inset pocket by putting the stitches where the pocket is to be placed onto a holder after working across them on the right side. Then you continue across the row to the end and place the lining as illustrated here. At the finishing stage, you can then work from the held stitches to create an edging, such as ribbing, seed stitch, or garter stitch.*

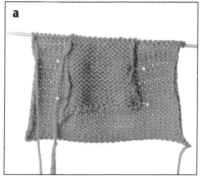

A *turned hem* creates a neat edge and can be used instead of ribbing at a hemline, a neck, on a cuff or along the button band on a cardigan. Usually, the part of the hem that is turned under to the wrong side is worked in a flat stitch such as stockinette, on smaller-size needles. A *turning row* is worked at the fold line to make a neat edge that folds easily.

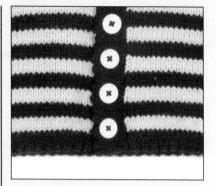

HEM WITH PURLED TURNING ROW

To knit a hem with a purled turning row, you knit the facing in stockinette stitch, on smaller needles than used for the project, to the desired length, and then you purl the turning row on the right side. You work the garment from there in the pattern, using the standard needle size being used for the project. When it is time to finish the garment, you fold over the hem at the purled row, and then you pin and stitch it in place.

HEM WITH PICOT TURNING ROW

This is a pretty hem that looks like a row of tiny scallops. It works well on dresses and baby clothes. You begin a hem with a picot turning row in a similar fashion to how you begin a hem with a purled turning row, only you form the picot turning row on an even number of stitches on the right side by working a knit 2 together, yarn over eyelet pattern across, ending with a single knit stitch. When you finish the garment, you fold the hem along the eyelet row and pin and stitch it in place.

PICOT TURNED BUTTON BAND

When using a picot hem to make a buttonhole band, you work the buttonholes symmetrically on either side of the turning row. You finish the band in the same manner as you would a hem, only you reinforce the buttonholes (see pages 164–165) through the two thicknesses.

If you're the type of knitter who enjoys minimal finishing, this hem is for you. It is created in a similar fashion to the hems shown on the opposite page, except that instead of sewing it in place at the finishing stage, you attach it by knitting the cast-on edge onto the main part of the garment.

How to Knit In a Hem

1 Work a 1-inch facing in stockinette stitch on a smaller needle than your project requires, as described on the opposite page, ending with a wrong side row.

2 Purl the next right side row to create the turning row.

3 Change to the needles used to knit the main part of your garment, and when you have worked 1 inch beyond the turning row, ending with a wrong side row, you are ready to knit in the hem.

4 With the right side facing, use a separate ball of yarn and the smaller needles you used to knit the hem facing to pick up stitches (see pages 152–155) along the cast-on edge, being sure to evenly pick up the same number of stitches that you have on the knitting needle for your garment. Cut the yarn used to pick up stitches, leaving a 6-inch tail.

5 Turn the hem so that the wrong side of the facing and the wrong side of your work are facing each other. Hold the knitting needles parallel to each other in your left hand, with the right side of your garment facing.

6 Insert the third needle, your working needle, into the first stitch on the front needle, then into the first stitch on the needle holding the picked-up stitches, and use your main working yarn to knit the 2 stitches as one; then slip them off the needles.

You should now have 1 stitch on the working needle.

7 Repeat step 6 across until you have knit together all the picked-up stitches and all the main garment stitches. Continue from here as established.

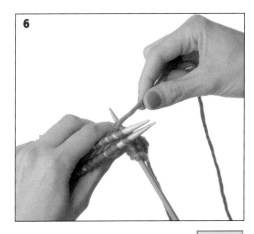

Decorative Details

To add something extra to a knitting project, you might want to embellish it with decorative touches. You can add a pompom to a hat, fringe to a scarf, or a tassel to a pillow cover. You can also add interest and color by embroidering directly onto your knitting. This chapter covers some basic finishing touches and embellishments that come up frequently in knitting patterns.

Make Pompoms

Pompoms add a nice touch to hats, scarves, and other projects. They are easy to make, and you can make them using one color or many.

To make pompoms, you can use a commercial pompom maker or materials you have in your home. In addition to yarn, you need flexible cardboard (shirt cardboard works well) and a pair of scissors.

The first method shown here creates a loose pompom, and the second method results in a firmer, rounder pompom.

How to Make a Loose Pompom

This method creates a loose pompom that can be left with loopy ends.

1. Cut a piece of cardboard into a rectangle whose width is the size you want your pompom to be. (So, for a 3-inch pompom, cut a piece of cardboard that's 3 inches wide.)

2. Wrap the yarn around the cardboard about 50 times.

3. Carefully remove the cardboard from the wrapped yarn.

④ Wrap a 12-inch strand of yarn tightly around the center of the yarn loops twice, and then tie it in a firm knot.

⑤ Cut the loops and fluff up the pompom to even it out.

Note: *You can leave the ends uncut for a loopy pompom.*

⑥ Use the tie ends to sew the pompom to your knitting.

CONTINUED ON NEXT PAGE

FAQ

I came across some patterns that use a technique called *felting*. What is felting, and is it difficult to do?

Felting is what can happen when you expose wool knits to moisture and heat. The knitting shrinks and becomes matted, looking like boiled wool slippers. Felting garments is tricky, as you need to knit your item large enough to allow for shrinkage. As a beginner, you can experiment with felting by using simple swatches. Put a wool swatch into the washing machine with a pair of canvas sneakers or denim pants and wash in hot water with a little bit of detergent. Wash for about five minutes, and then check to see if your swatch has felted. It will shrink quickly, so don't leave it in for the whole cycle. When the swatch has felted, remove it from the wash, rinse in cool water, and lay it flat to dry.

How to Make a Tight Pompom

With this method you can create a firm, round pompom.

1 Cut two pieces of cardboard into circles the same size you want your pompom to be. Cut a pie piece out of each circle, then cut a circle out of the center of each of the circles. The two pieces should be identical.

2 Match up the two cardboard pieces, one on top of the other, and wrap the yarn around them tightly and densely, as shown. Cut the yarn end.

Note: Use less yarn for a loose pompom and more yarn for a dense pompom.

3 Insert scissors between the two circles and under the yarn, as shown. Cut the yarn all the way around the outside of the cardboard circles.

4. Bring a strand of yarn—at least 12 inches long—between the two cardboard pieces and around the center of the cut yarns. Tie it very tightly in a square knot.

5. Remove the cardboard pieces.

6. Trim the edges of the pompom to make it nice and round.

7. Use the yarn ends from tying the pompom to attach the pompom to your project.

Make Tassels

You can embellish pillows, baby blankets, hats, and scarves with tassels. They are very easy to make, and, like pompoms, can be made in one color or in two or more colors.

To make a tassel, you need a piece of rigid cardboard, a pair of scissors, a tapestry needle, and yarn.

How to Make a Tassel

① Cut the cardboard into a rectangle that is the same length you want your tassel to be. (So, for a 6-inch-long tassel, cut a piece of cardboard that's 6 inches long.)

② Wrap the yarn around the cardboard to the desired thickness.

Note: *Thin yarn requires more wraps than thick yarn.*

③ Thread a tapestry needle with a 12-inch strand of the same yarn used for the tassel and insert the needle between the cardboard and the wrapped strands. Pull the yarn all the way through.

④ Separate the tapestry needle from the yarn and tie the strand's ends together tightly in a knot at the top edge of the cardboard to secure the tassel.

5 Insert scissors between the wrapped strands and the cardboard at the opposite end from the tied end and cut the tassel free along the bottom edge of the cardboard.

6 Wrap a 10-inch strand of yarn around the tassel a few times, about ½ inch down from the tied end; then tie the ends tightly in a knot.

Note: *You can use the same color yarn or an accent color for step 6.*

7 Conceal the yarn ends from step 6 by threading them through a tapestry needle and inserting the needle back into the tassel near the top. Pull the tapestry needle out at the tassel end.

8 Trim the tassel ends to neaten them.

9 Use the tail coming out of the top of the tassel to sew it onto your knitting project.

Add Fringe

Fringe works well on scarves, throws, sweater hems, and ponchos. You can make fringe with all kinds of yarn. Combining two or more different colors or types of yarn to make fringe can have a lovely effect, so experiment by holding various yarn odds and ends together to see how they look.

To make fringe, you need yarn, a pair of scissors, and a crochet hook.

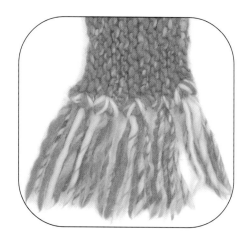

How to Add Fringe

Fringe can use up a fair amount of yarn, so make sure you have enough before you begin. Fringe made of thick yarn requires fewer strands of yarn than fringe made with thin yarn. Experiment with different thicknesses to see what works best for your particular project.

1. Determine how long you want your final fringe to be. Then cut yarn to double that length, plus an inch extra for the knot.

2. Hold the strands together, with the ends matched up, creating a loop at the top.

3. Hold your knitting with the right side facing you. Insert the crochet hook from back to front into the lower-left corner, just above the cast-on row.

4. Use the crochet hook to take hold of your loop of folded strands.

⑤ Use the crochet hook to pull the strands through from front to back.

⑥ Pull the loop from under the cast-on row and insert the fringe ends down into the loop and tighten.

⑦ Repeat steps 2–6 across the base of your knitting to complete the fringe.

⑧ When you have finished attaching the fringe, trim it with scissors so that it is even.

Knit a Cord

You can knit tubular cords and put them to all sorts of decorative uses. Knitted cords make excellent handles for a bag; they can also be looped and configured to make floral hat toppers. Or, instead of using fringe on scarf ends, you can attach knitted cords.

Knitting a cord is like knitting in the round on a tiny scale. You need two double-pointed needles suitably sized for your yarn.

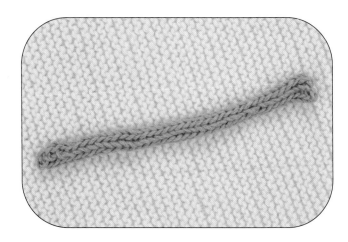

How to Knit a Cord

1. Cast on 5 or 6 stitches onto one of your dpns (double-pointed needles).
2. Knit across the stitches but do not turn your work.

3. Push the stitches back to the other end of the dpn, so you're ready to work a right side row again. Insert the second dpn into the first stitch to knit as usual, firmly pull the working yarn from the end of the row, and knit.

   Note: Beginning the row (round, actually) by pulling the yarn from the opposite end closes the tube.

4. Repeat steps 2 and 3 until the cord is the desired length. Bind off or cut the yarn and pull it through all the stitches to tighten.

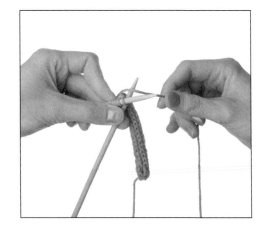

Make a Twisted Cord

A twisted cord is an easy-to-make embellishment that can serve several purposes. Twisted cords not only make perfect mitten chains, but they also work well as straps for bags. You can attach pompoms or tassels to the end of a twisted cord for an added effect on hat or sweater ties.

You can twist two or more colors or yarn types together for a more colorful or textural cord.

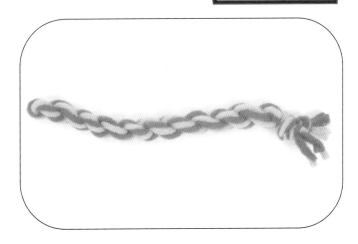

How to Make a Twisted Cord

The thickness of a twisted cord depends on the thickness of the yarn and on the number of strands twisted together. If the cord will be used to bear weight, be sure to make it thick.

1️⃣ Determine how long you want your twisted cord to be. Then cut a few strands of yarn three times that length. Knot the strands together at each end.

2️⃣ Insert a knitting needle at each knotted end and pull the strands taut. Twist one of the needles in a clockwise motion until the strands are tightly spun together.

Note: If your strands are longer than your arm span, anchor one knotted end on a coat hook, a doorknob, or another stationary object.

3️⃣ Maintaining tight tension on the strands, and taking care not to let them untwist, fold the strands in half—holding the fold loop firmly in one hand—so that the knotted ends are lined up with each other. Let go of the ends, and the cord twists itself together, forming an elegant rope.

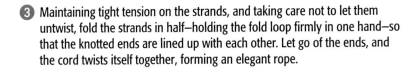

Decorate with Embroidery

You can decorate your knitting with embroidery stitches. You do this after you have blocked your work. Embroidered edgings, such as whipstitch and blanket stitch, add color and detail to casual knits, baby blankets, and scarves. Embroidered motifs look best on flat stitch patterns, such as garter stitch or stockinette stitch. You can use yarn or embroidery floss to embroider on your knitting.

Embroidery Stitches

STRAIGHT STITCH

Straight stitch is a good drawing stitch, and it's the easiest to do. Straight stitch adds a nice accent along hems and pockets.

1. Thread a tapestry needle with the yarn you want to embroider with. Tie a knot in the yarn end about 6 inches up from the bottom. Bring the threaded needle up through the knitting from back to front, until the knot stops it.

2. Lay the needle flat with the knitting and insert it 1 stitch length from where it came out; reinsert the tip from underneath so that it comes back out 1 stitch length from the second insertion. Pull the yarn all the way through.

3. Continue weaving the needle in and out to create straight stitch. You can weave in and out several times in one step to create a few stitches at once.

4. When you're finished, pull the yarn through to the wrong side, knot it, and weave in the end.

WHIPSTITCH

Whipstitch adds a homey touch to edges and is one of the easiest and most basic stitches you can use.

1. Thread a tapestry needle with the yarn you want to embroider with. Tie a knot in the yarn end about 6 inches up from the bottom. Bring the threaded needle up through the knitting from back to front, until the knot stops it.

2. Bring the tapestry needle in and out from back to front up the side of the knitting.

3. When you're finished, pull the yarn through to the wrong side, knot it, and weave in the end.

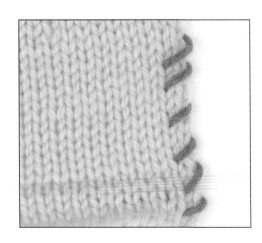

BLANKET STITCH

Blanket stitch is just like buttonhole stitch (see page 165), but you can do it on a larger scale to create an edging. Blanket stitch adds a rustic feel to sweaters, blankets, and scarves.

1 Thread a tapestry needle with the yarn you want to embroider with. Tie a knot in the yarn end about 6 inches up from the bottom. Bring the needle through at the edge of your knitting from back to front, pulling the yarn through until the knot stops it.

2 Moving right to left, insert the needle at the desired depth into the edge and bring it out again to the front, as shown, taking care that the needle tip overlaps the yarn coming out of the starting point.

3 Repeat step 2 along the edge of your knitting to create blanket stitch. When you are done, weave in the yarn end.

DUPLICATE STITCH

This is a fun stitch that duplicates the knit stitch—the V—right on top of it. You can use this stitch to create motifs that look knit in.

1 Thread a tapestry needle with the yarn you want to embroider with. Bring the needle through the knitting at the hole just below the V that you want to duplicate. Pull the yarn through, leaving a 6-inch tail.

2 Insert the needle from right to left under both loops of the V above the stitch you want to duplicate; pull the yarn through all the way.

3 Reinsert the needle into the hole below your stitch—the same hole that the needle came through in step 1—and bring it out again below the next stitch to be worked, all in one movement.

4 Repeat steps 2 and 3 to create duplicate stitch. When you are done, weave in the loose ends.

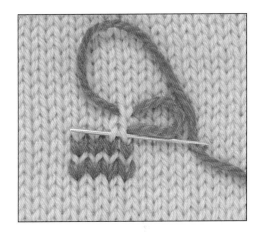

CHAIN STITCH

Chain stitch looks like a line of loops. It works well on edgings such as collars and pockets, and it can be used as an outline for decorative motifs.

1 Thread a tapestry needle with the yarn you want to embroider with. Bring the needle through from back to front, pulling the yarn through and leaving a 6-inch tail at the back.

2 Hold the yarn in a loop, as shown. Reinsert the needle right next to where it came out in step 1; bring the needle back out over the loop a small stitch away.

3 Repeat step 2 to create chain stitch. When you are done, weave in the yarn end.

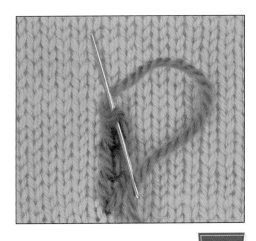

CONTINUED ON NEXT PAGE

CROSS-STITCH

Cross-stitch gives your work the old-fashioned look of an embroidery sampler.

1 Thread a tapestry needle with the yarn you want to embroider with. Pull the needle through from back to front, at the point that will be the lower-right corner of the X, leaving a 6-inch tail of yarn at the back.

2 Insert the needle from front to back into the point that will be the upper-left corner of the X, making one diagonal straight stitch. Pull the thread all the way through but don't pull it too tight.

3 Insert the needle from back to front at the point that will be the upper-right corner of the X and pull the yarn through all the way.

4 End the X by inserting the needle from the front at the point that will be the lower-left corner of the X and pull the yarn through all the way.

5 Repeat steps 1–4 for cross-stitch. When you are done, weave in the yarn end.

STEM STITCH

This is good for outlining and also makes a nice stem for embroidered flowers.

1 Thread a tapestry needle with the yarn you want to embroider with. Make a ¼-inch straight stitch to start, leaving a 6-inch tail of thread at the back of your work.

2 Bring the needle back through from back to front just next to the center of the stitch you made in step 1.

3 Holding the yarn with your left thumb above the point where it just came through, reinsert the needle about ¼-inch to the right of the first stitch, bringing the needle out at the end point of the first stitch.

4 Repeat step 3 to create stem stitch. When you are done, weave in the yarn end.

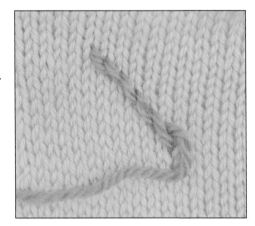

SATIN STITCH

Satin stitch is a series of straight stitches used to fill in outlines. Take care not to pull your stitches too tightly, or your knitting will pucker.

1 Thread a tapestry needle with the yarn you want to embroider with. Tie a knot in the yarn end about 6 inches up from the bottom.

2 To begin, insert the needle from back to front, pulling the yarn through until the knot stops it. Work a series of side-by-side straight stitches, varying the length to suit the outline of the motif you're filling.

3 When you are done, weave in the yarn end.

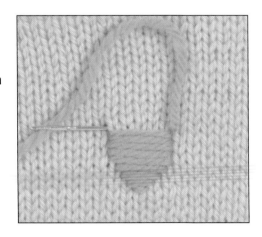

COUCHING STITCH

Couching stitch is achieved by laying yarn or thread onto your fabric in the shape or design you want and then whipstitching it in place with a second, thinner, yarn or thread. It results in colorful, playful outlines.

1. Begin by arranging the thicker thread on your knitting in the shape or line you want it to ultimately be.

2. Whipstitch it in place, using a needle threaded with a thinner yarn.

3. When you are done, weave in the yarn end.

FRENCH KNOT

You can use French knots for infinite purposes: as the centers of lazy daisies, as eyes, or as accents along a line at a border. They add a nice three-dimensional effect to your embroidery.

1. Thread a tapestry needle with the yarn you want to embroider with. Tie a knot in the yarn 6 inches up from the end. Bring the needle through the knitting from back to front, pulling through until the knot stops it.

2. Grasp the yarn about 1 inch above the point where it came out and wind the yarn around the tip of the needle three times, moving from the eye of the needle to the tip, as shown.

3. Still grasping the wound yarn, reinsert the needle right next to the point where it came out and pull it through all the way to the back to create the knot.

You have made one French knot.

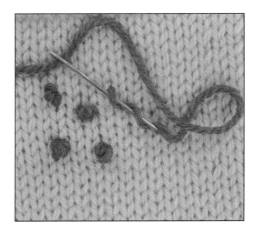

LAZY DAISY STITCH

You can use lazy daisy stitch to embroider flowers onto your knitting. You work it the same way as chain stitch, but not in a line. After making the petals, you can use a contrast color to embroider a French knot in the center.

1. Work one chain stitch as described on page 189, but instead of bringing the needle back into the stitch, insert it just below the loop of the chain, bringing it back out to the front, above the stitch, as shown.

You have made one daisy petal.

2. Repeat step 1 in a circle, until you have completed the daisy. When you are done, weave in the yarn end.

Note: You can use satin stitch to fill in the petals, if desired.

Crochet Edgings

You don't have be a crochet expert to finish your knitting with simple crochet edgings or chains. A crochet edge can not only neaten and firm up an unstable or curling edge, but it also adds interest and color to a plain-looking piece of knitting.

To crochet, you need yarn and a crochet hook that is the correct size for the yarn you're using.

How to Crochet a Chain

Chain stitch in crochet is the equivalent of casting on in knitting: It creates the foundation row of stitches from which to work. When you're working crochet directly onto your knitting, you don't necessarily need this foundation row. However, knowing how to work a chain will enable you not only to make decorative cords but also to incorporate button loops and picot trim into your crochet edgings.

Crochet instructions generally indicate working chain stitch by using the abbreviation *ch* followed by the number of chain stitches to make. For example, instructions to chain 3 read *ch3*.

1. Make a slipknot, leaving a 6-inch tail. Insert a crochet hook of an appropriate size for the yarn into the slipknot.

2. Wrap the working yarn around the crochet hook from back to front (creating a yarn over loop) so that the hook catches the yarn.

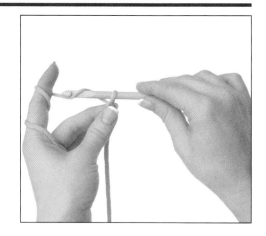

3. Holding the working yarn in your left hand and the hook in your right, pull the yarn over loop on the hook through the slipknot.

   You have made 1 loop in a chain.

4. Repeat steps 2 and 3 until the chain is the desired length. Cut the yarn, leaving a 6-inch tail, and pull it snugly through the last loop to finish the chain.

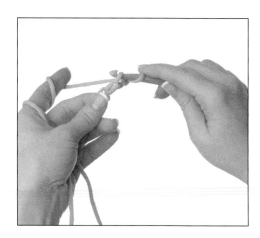

Slip Stitch Edging

You can slip stitch along an edge as a decorative touch, or as a base row underneath a second row of crochet. You work this edging from right to left.

Crochet instructions indicate slip stitch by using the abbreviation *sl st* followed by the number of slip stitches to make.

① Choose a crochet hook that is one or two sizes smaller than the needles used for your knitting. Insert the hook into your knitting at the right corner of the edge.

② Loop the yarn around the hook (yarn over) and pull the loop through.

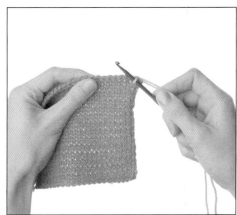

③ Insert the crochet hook into the next stitch of the knitting, yarn over again, and pull the loop through both the knitting and the loop on the hook from step 1.

You should now have 1 loop remaining on the hook.

④ Repeat step 3 across the edge. Cut the yarn and pull it snugly through the last loop to finish the edging.

Note: If a crochet edge is causing your knitting to flare and stretch, try a smaller hook or try skipping a stitch on the knitting every so often. If the edge is too tight, try a larger hook or try crocheting with a looser touch.

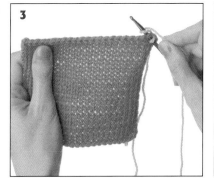

CONTINUED ON NEXT PAGE

Single Crochet Edging

Single crochet provides a neat, firm edge that is a little more substantial than a slip stitch edge. You work this edging from right to left.

Crochet instructions indicate single crochet by using the abbreviation *sc* followed by the number of single crochet stitches you should make.

1 Choose a crochet hook that is one or two sizes smaller than the needles used for your knitting. Insert the hook into your knitting at the right corner of the edge.

2 Loop the yarn around the hook (yarn over) and pull the loop through.

3 Working from the front, yarn over and pull a new loop through the first loop.

4 Insert the crochet hook into the next stitch to the left on the knitting, yarn over, and pull a new loop through.

You should now have 2 loops on the crochet hook.

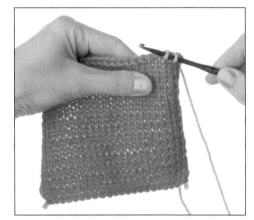

5 Yarn over the crochet hook again and pull this new loop through both loops already on the hook.

6 Repeat steps 4 and 5 across the edge. Cut the yarn and pull it through the last loop to finish the edging.

Picot Edging

Crocheting a picot edging makes a fancy edge that looks great on feminine sweaters and baby knits.

1 Choose a crochet hook that is one or two sizes smaller than the needles used for your knitting. Insert the hook into your knitting at the right corner of the edge.

2 Work 1 single crochet (see steps 2–5 on page 194).

3 Chain 3 (or 4, if desired).

4 Insert the crochet hook back into the same stitch, yarn over, and bring up a loop.

5 Yarn over again and pull the loop through both loops on the hook.

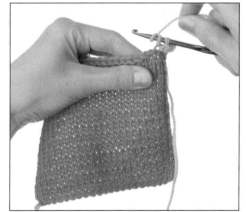

6 Single crochet 2 (into the next 2 stitches, moving left).

7 Repeat steps 2–5 across the edge to create picot edging. Cut the yarn and pull it snugly through the last loop to finish the edging.

Note: *To create more space between picots, you can single crochet 3 or 4 times at step 5.*

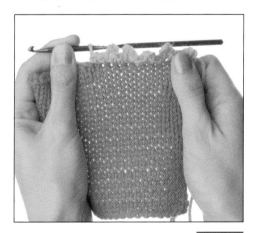

Knit Fancy Borders and Edgings

Sometimes a plain sweater needs to be dressed up a little. You can work a fancy ruffle or border at the edge to add that accent to your knitting. The following ruffles, borders, and edgings are all easy to create. You can work them in the same color as your knitting or in an accent color.

How to Make Ruffles

BASIC RUFFLE

For this ruffle, you need to start with twice the number of stitches as there are in the main part of your knitting. For example, if you are knitting a sweater back over 60 stitches, you cast on 120 for this ruffle. You work this basic ruffle over an even number of stitches.

1 Cast on twice the number of sts that you want to end up with.

2 Work in St st to the desired length of the ruffle, ending with a purl row.

3 K2tog across the entire row. You end up with half the number of sts you cast on.

Note: You can work 3 rows of garter stitch to reinforce the decrease row.

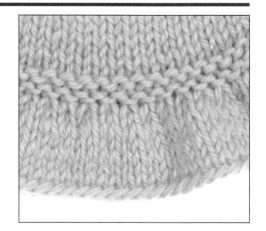

CURLY RUFFLE

This is a fun ruffle that looks great on baby blankets and little girls' sweaters. You need to cast on four times the number of stitches you want to end up with, minus 3. For example, if you want to end up with 60 stitches, you cast on 237 stitches to create a curly ruffle. You work this border on a multiple of 2 stitches plus 1.

1 Row 1 (RS): K1, *k2, pass the first of these 2 sts over the second and off the needle; rep from * to end of row.

2 Row 2 (WS): P1, *p2tog; rep from * to end of row.

Note: You can work the ruffle on smaller needles if you want it to be tighter.

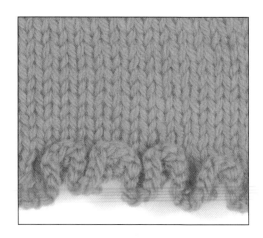

How to Make Borders

BOBBLED BORDER

You work this border, which creates a nice three-dimensional edge, on a multiple of 6 stitches plus 5.

To make bobble (mb): Work to the point where you want the bobble. Knit into the front, back, front, back, and front (that's five times) of the next stitch. Without turning the work, use the left needle to pick up the fourth stitch and pass it over the fifth and off the needle; pass the third over the fifth and off; pass the second over the fifth and off; and finally, pass the first over the fifth stitch and off.

1. Row 1 (WS): Knit.
2. Row 2 (RS–bobble row): K2, *mb, k5; rep from * to last 3 sts, mb, k2.
3. Rows 3–5: Knit.

MINI SCALLOPS

This is a pretty little edging that is easy to do. It adds a delicate touch to feminine sweaters or baby blankets. You work this border on a multiple of 5 stitches plus 2.

1. Row 1 (RS): K1, yo, *k5, [pass the second, third, fourth, and fifth sts over the first st and off], yo; rep from * to last st, k1.

   You now have a multiple of 2 sts plus 3 on your needle.
2. Row 2 (WS): P1, *[p1, yo, k1 tbl] all in next st, p1; rep from * to end of row.

   You now have a multiple of 4 sts plus 1 on your needle.
3. Row 3: K2, k1 tbl, *k3, k1 tbl; rep from * to last 2 sts, k2.
4. Rows 4–6: Knit.

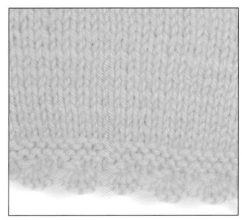

EASY POINTED BORDER

This border creates a series of diagonally biased points. You make the border as long as the edge you need to attach it to and sew it on later. To create this border, cast on 6 stitches.

1. Row 1 (RS): K3, yo, k3—7 sts.
2. Rows 2, 4, 6, 8, and 10 (WS): Knit.
3. Row 3: K3, yo, k4—8 sts.
4. Row 5: K3, yo, k5—9 sts.
5. Row 7: K3, yo, k6—10 sts.
6. Row 9: K3, yo, k7—11 sts.
7. Row 11: K3, yo, k8—12 sts.
8. Row 12: Bind off 6 sts, k5—6 sts.
9. Repeat rows 1–12 until the edging is the desired length. Bind off all stitches.

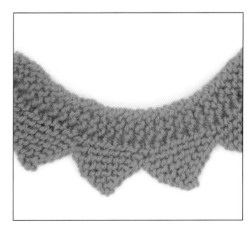

Knit with Beads

Knitting beads directly into your work is an embellishment that can have varied effects. You can create elegant purses and eveningwear by knitting delicate glass beads with fine yarns, or you can create a more casual look by knitting wooden beads into a thick, sturdy, natural-looking yarn. Since beading has grown in popularity, you can find a wide selection of beads at large craft stores. Be sure that your beads and yarn have compatible care instructions.

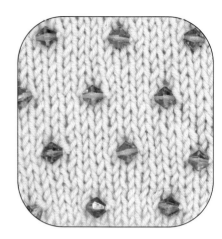

How to Knit with Beads

To knit with beads, you must thread all the beads directly onto your ball of working yarn before beginning to knit. You need to make sure that the beads you're using are suited to your yarn visually and in terms of size. The beads should slide along the yarn with ease. This beaded sample is worked on the right side of stockinette stitch.

1 Thread the end of the working yarn into a needle that is small enough to fit through the hole in the bead. Thread all the beads you will need onto the working yarn, sliding them down toward the yarn ball.

2 Cast on stitches and work your knitting pattern's instructions.

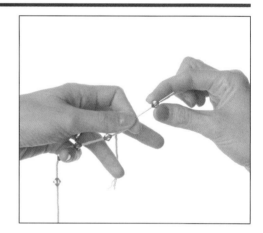

3 When you get to the point on a right side row where you're ready to add a bead, bring the working yarn to the front, between your needles.

4 Slide the first bead up the yarn so that it rests snugly against the last knit stitch.

5 Use the tip of the right needle to slip the next stitch on the left needle knitwise to the right needle.

6 Bring the working yarn to the back, adjust the bead so that it is placed where you want it, and knit the next stitch snugly to hold the bead firmly in place.

You have beaded 1 stitch.

FAQ

I want to use very small beads but am finding it hard to get a threaded needle through the hole. Is there another method I can use to thread the beads onto the yarn?

Yes, as long as your yarn is not so thick that it can't be threaded into the hole of the bead at all. To thread tiny beads onto fine yarn, you can use a beading needle threaded with thin thread to bring your yarn through the hole. Simply loop the thread around a fold in your yarn and then insert both ends of the thread into the eye of the needle. Slide the bead over the needle and then pull the needle, the thread, and the yarn through the bead hole.

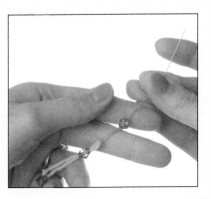

Easy Knitting Projects

The projects in this chapter introduce you to some basic techniques, without overwhelming you with elaborate shaping, construction, or stitch patterns. It's good to make your first project a short one, so that you achieve the satisfaction of finishing something quickly. Be sure to refer to earlier chapters to review how-to information, if necessary.

Easy Horizontal Scarf

You knit this scarf the long way, casting on a lot of stitches onto a long circular needle. It knits up very quickly that way, especially at 3 stitches per inch. Because this scarf is knit in simple garter stitch, you should use a yarn that is rich and varied on its own, like this beautiful hand-spun wool. It's a good idea to test the yarn against your neck to make sure it is soft and not itchy.

Specifications

SIZE

72 inches (not including fringe) x 4 inches

MATERIALS

2 hanks Muench Yarns/Naturwolle *Black Forest Soft* (100% hand-spun wool, 110 yards/100g hank) in red #08

Small amount of accent yarn for fringe (sample used a combination of the scarf yarn and Muench Yarns/Naturwolle *Black Forest Tweed* in yellow T2-08)

Size 13 (9mm) circular needle, at least 29 inches long

Tapestry needle

Size K (6.5mm) crochet hook

GAUGE

12 stitches and 22 rows to 4 inches over garter stitch on size 13 (9mm) needles

SCARF

1 CO 215 sts.

2 Work in garter st (knit every row) until the scarf is the desired width, making sure you have enough yarn left to BO (that is, at least four times the length of the scarf). (The sample shown was knit to 4 inches in width and used almost two full hanks of Naturwolle *Black Forest Soft*.)

3 BO sts at an even tension. Cut yarn, leaving a 6-inch tail, and pull tail through last st to secure.

FINISHING

1 Weave in ends.

> *Note: Because a scarf is viewed on both sides, take care to weave in ends as inconspicuously as possible.*

2 Block the scarf so that the edges are even. (See pages 138–139.)

3 To make fringe, cut four 12-inch strands of yarn for each bunch of fringe. Add five bunches of fringe to each end of the scarf, using a crochet hook. (See pages 184–185 for instructions on finishing with fringe.)

Striped Baby Blanket

This is an easy project that gets you started on changing colors in stockinette stitch. It is a cheery blanket that makes a good baby gift. Be sure to use a yarn that is machine washable. The blanket shown has a single crochet edge, which not only adds color but also helps to uncurl the edges. However, if you're not ready to try crochet, you can instead whipstitch (see page 186) the edge in a contrast color.

Specifications

SIZE

30 inches x 28 inches

MATERIALS

5 balls Muench Yarns/GGH *Goa* (50% cotton/50% acrylic, 66 yards/50g ball) in green #31 (A), 4 balls in yellow #39 (B), and 1 ball in red #07 (C)

Size 10 (6mm) circular needle, at least 29 inches long

Size J (6mm) crochet hook

Tapestry needle

GAUGE

14 stitches and 19 rows to 4 inches over stockinette stitch on size 10 (6mm) needles

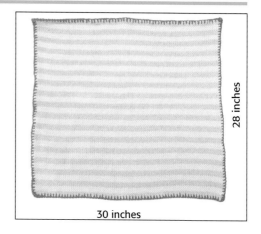

28 inches

30 inches

Pattern Stitch

STRIPE PATTERN

Work stripe patt in St st (knit on RS, purl on WS) as follows:

4 rows in green
4 rows in yellow

Note: *If you want to avoid having to weave in so many ends, you can carry the colors alternately up the side as you go (see page 118).*

How to Make the Striped Baby Blanket

BLANKET

① CO 99 sts in A.

② Beg with a knit row, work in stripe pattern until you have worked 33 stripes total (17 green stripes and 16 yellow stripes).

③ BO sts. Cut yarn and pull tail through last st to secure.

FINISHING

① Weave in ends.

② Lightly steam on WS to block and reduce curling.

③ Single crochet (see page 194) in C around perimeter of blanket. Weave in these ends and lightly steam edges again.

Washcloth Set

Making these two washcloths allows you to practice some textured stitch patterns without having to worry about shaping at the same time. The finished set, tied with a ribbon, makes a nice gift.

SIZE

10 inches x 10 inches

MATERIALS

1 ball each Muench Yarns/GGH *Goa* (50% cotton/50% acrylic, 66 yards/50g ball) in blue #13 (A) and taupe #30 (B)

Size 10 (6mm) needles

Tapestry needle

GAUGE

14 stitches and 19 rows to 4 inches over stockinette stitch on size 10 (6mm) needles

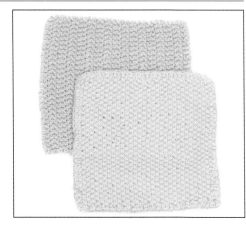

Pattern Stitches

GARTER RIB (MULT OF 4 STS PLUS 2)

All rows: K2, *p2, k2; rep from * to end.

SEED STITCH (EVEN NUMBER OF STS)

Row 1 (RS): *K1, p1; rep from * to end.

Row 2 (WS): *P1, k1; rep from * to end.

Rep rows 1 and 2 for seed st.

How to Make the Washcloth Set

WASHCLOTH IN GARTER RIB

1 CO 34 sts in A.

2 Work in garter rib until piece measures approx 10 inches from beg.

3 BO sts in patt.

FINISHING

1 Weave in ends.

2 Thread a tapestry needle with B and embroider the perimeter of the cloth in whipstitch (see page 188).

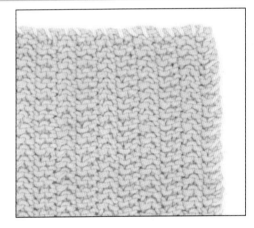

WASHCLOTH IN SEED STITCH

1 CO 34 sts in B.

2 Work in seed st until piece measures approx 10 inches from beg.

3 BO sts in patt.

FINISHING

1 Weave in ends.

2 Thread a tapestry needle with A and embroider the perimeter of the cloth in blanket stitch (see page 189).

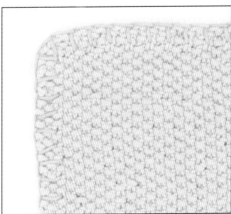

Wrist Warmers

Here is another quick and easy project. These are simply rectangles worked in a seeded rib. After you finish the knitting, you sew the rectangles up the side, leaving a hole for the thumb. The seeded rib results in a highly fluted, three-dimensional texture. Try wearing them over mittens or gloves for added warmth.

Specifications

SIZE

7½ inches x 9½ inches

MATERIALS

1 hank Cascade Yarns *Pastaza* (50% llama/50% wool, 132 yards/100g hank) in yellow #78

Size 11 (8mm) needles

Tapestry needle

GAUGE

12 stitches and 16 rows to 4 inches over seeded rib pattern on size 11 (8mm) needles

Note: *The generic gauge for this yarn is actually 4 stitches per inch over stockinette stitch on size 9 (5.5mm) needles. Larger needles are used for this project to accentuate the open stitch pattern.*

Pattern Stitch

SEEDED RIB (MULT OF 4 STS PLUS 1)

Row 1 (RS): P1, *k3, p1; rep from * to end.

Row 2 (WS): K2, p1, *k3, p1; rep from * to last 2 sts, end k2.

Rep rows 1 and 2 for seeded rib.

How to Make the Wrist Warmers

WRIST WARMERS

1. CO 29 sts, leaving a tail to sew seam.

2. Work in seeded rib until piece measures approx 7½ inches, ending with a RS row.

3. BO sts in patt on WS row, leaving another tail to sew seam from that end.

FINISHING

1. Do not block. Sew seam for 4 inches from one end. Sew seam for 1¾ inches from other end, leaving a 1¾-inch hole for thumb.

2. Weave in ends.

Tweedy Pointed Hat

This hat is worked in a beautiful hand-spun yarn that, at 3 stitches per inch, knits up very quickly. The pointed top results from working a progression of decreases every other row so that the shaping is gradual. Instructions for both knitting the hat flat and in the round are included. The sizes listed should cover the whole family.

Specifications

SIZES

S (M, L)

Brim circumference: 16 (18, 20) inches

MATERIALS

1 hank Muench Yarns/Naturwolle Black Forest *Tweed* (100% hand-spun wool, 110 yards/100g hank) in black/white tweed #T5-191

Or

1 hank yellow/red tweed #T2-08

Pair of size 13 (9mm) straight needles, if working flat

Set of four size 13 (9mm) double-pointed needles, if working in the round

Stitch marker, if working in the round

Tapestry needle

Size J (6mm) crochet hook

GAUGE

12 stitches and 18 rows (or rounds) to 4 inches over stockinette stitch on size 13 (9mm) needles

How to Make the Tweedy Pointed Hat on Straight Needles

HAT BODY

1 CO 48 (54, 60) sts on straight needles.

2 Beg with a knit row, work in St st (knit on RS, purl on WS) for 4¾ (5½, 6¼) inches, ending with a WS row.

SHAPE TOP

Note: *In this pattern you decrease by using k2tog (see page 54).*

1 Row 1 (RS): *K6 (7, 8), k2tog; rep from * to end—42 (48, 54) sts.

2 Row 2 and all rem WS rows: Purl.

3 Row 3: *K5 (6, 7), k2tog; rep from * to end—36 (42, 48) sts.

4 Row 5: *K4 (5, 6), k2tog; rep from * to end—30 (36, 42) sts.

5 Row 7: *K3 (4, 5), k2tog; rep from * to end—24 (30, 36) sts.

6 Row 9: *K2 (3, 4), k2tog; rep from * to end—18 (24, 30) sts.

7 Row 11: *K1 (2, 3), k2tog; rep from * to end—12 (18, 24) sts.

8 Row 13: *K0 (1, 2), k2tog; rep from * to end—6 (12, 18) sts.

9 Row 15: *K0 (0, 1), k2tog; rep from * to end—3 (6, 12) sts.

10 Row 17 *(M and L only)*: K2tog across—3 (6) sts.

11 Row 19 *(L only)*: K2tog across—3 sts.

FINISHING

1 Cut yarn, leaving a 24-inch tail. Pull tail through last 3 sts and secure.

2 Steam piece to block.

3 Use tail to sew back seam. Weave in ends.

4 Single crochet around brim to flatten and firm. Weave in rem loose ends.

5 Steam seam and brim to finish.

CONTINUED ON NEXT PAGE

How to Make the Tweedy Pointed Hat in the Round

HAT BODY

1. CO 48 (54, 60) sts, dividing sts evenly over three dpns.

2. Place marker for beg of rnd, join rnd, taking care not to twist sts, and knit every rnd until hat measures 4¾ (5½, 6¼) inches from beg.

SHAPE TOP

Note: In this pattern you decrease by using k2tog (see page 54).

1. Round 1: *K6 (7, 8), k2tog; rep from * to end of rnd—42 (48, 54) sts.

2. Round 2: Knit.

3. Round 3: *K5 (6, 7), k2tog; rep from * to end of rnd—36 (42, 48) sts.

4. Round 4: Knit.

5. Round 5: *K4 (5, 6), k2tog; rep from * to end of rnd—30 (36, 42) sts.

6. Continue as established, dec 6 sts, evenly spaced, every other rnd until 12 sts rem. Knit 1 rnd.

7. Next round: K2tog around—6 sts.

8. Knit 1 rnd.

9. Last round: K2tog around—3 sts.

FINISHING

1. Cut yarn, leaving an 8-inch tail. Pull tail through last 3 sts and secure.

2. Weave in end at brim, using it to secure the joining of the first rnd, if necessary.

3. Steam hat to block.

4. Beg at joining of first rnd, single crochet edge to flatten and firm brim. Weave in rem ends.

5. Steam crochet edge to finish.

Dropped Stitch Scarf

This openwork scarf is so easy and works up so quickly that you can finish the whole project in just a few hours. Using larger needles than the yarn calls for makes for a very airy fabric with a lot of drape. This particular scarf is short so that the pompoms rest near the neck, but you can make it as long as you like.

Specifications

SIZE

30 inches x 8½ inches

MATERIALS

1 hank Cascade Yarns *Pastaza* (50% llama/50% wool, 132 yards/100g hank) in yellow #78

Size 15 (10mm) needles

Tapestry needle

Pompom maker or cardboard

GAUGE

7 stitches and 8 rows to 4 inches over dropped stitch garter on size 15 (10mm) needles

Note: *The generic gauge for this yarn is actually 4 stitches per inch over stockinette stitch on size 9 (5.5mm) needles. Larger needles are used for this project to accentuate the open stitch pattern.*

CONTINUED ON NEXT PAGE

Pattern Stitch

DROPPED STITCH GARTER PATTERN

Rows 1 and 2: Knit.

Row 3: K1, *yo twice, k1; rep from * to end.

Row 4: Knit across, dropping the yo loops as you go.

Rep rows 1–4 for dropped stitch garter.

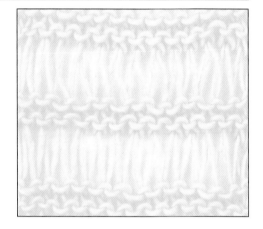

How to Make the Dropped Stitch Scarf

SCARF

1. CO 15 sts, leaving a 10-inch tail.

2. Work in dropped stitch garter pattern until scarf measures 30 inches (or desired length), ending with row 1 or 2 of pattern.

3. BO sts, leaving a 10-inch tail.

FINISHING

1. Weave in the cast-on tail and the bind-off tail, using them to gather the ends of the scarf.

2. Make two 2¼-inch tight pompoms. (See page 180 for instructions.)

3. Gather the ends of the scarf and sew the pompoms to the ends to hold the gathers.

Here is an easy hat that gives you some practice with striped ribbing. The samples shown have a vintage look and are knit in a very soft alpaca, so they don't itch. Because the style is unisex and the size range is broad, you can make this hat for just about anyone. You can add a pompom (see pages 178–181) if you like.

Specifications

SIZES

XS (S, M, L)

Brim circumference: 14¾ (16½, 18, 20) inches

MATERIALS

1 ball each elann.com's *Peruvian Collection Pure Alpaca* (100% alpaca, 109 yards/50g ball) in brown #205 (A) and pink #2170 (B)

Or

1 ball each blue #9155 (A) and brown #205 (B)

Pair of size 6 (4mm) needles

Tapestry needle

GAUGE

20 stitches and 25 rows to 4 inches over stockinette stitch on size 6 (4mm) needles

Note: *If your row gauge is off, the hat may come out too short or too long. To compensate, add or subtract rows from the first and last stripes.*

Pattern Stitches

RIB PATTERN

Row 1 (RS): K2, *p2, k2; rep from * to end.

Row 2 (WS): P2, *k2, p2; rep from * to end.

Note: *Make color changes on RS rows. Be sure to knit only across the first row of the new stripe when changing colors to ensure a smooth color break. (This will not disrupt the rib.)*

CONTINUED ON NEXT PAGE

How to Make the Striped Rib Hat

HAT BODY

1 CO 74 (82, 90, 98) sts in A.

2 Beg with row 1, work in rib patt and, AT THE SAME TIME, work stripe patt, as follows:

10 (10, 12, 14) rows in A

2 rows in B

8 rows in A

4 (6, 6, 8) rows in B

4 (6, 6, 8) rows in A

8 rows in B

2 rows in A

2 rows in B

SHAPE TOP

Note: Work in B for rem of hat.

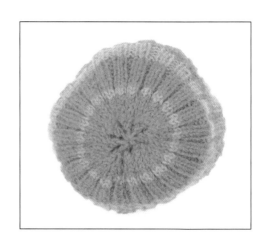

1 Row 1 (RS): Still using B, k2, *p2tog, k2; rep from * to end—56 (62, 68, 74) sts.

2 Row 2 (WS): P2, *k1, p2; rep from * to end.

3 Row 3: K2tog, *p1, K2tog; rep from * to end—37 (41, 45, 49) sts.

4 Row 4: *P3tog; rep from * across, end p1 (2, 0, 1)—13 (15, 15, 17) sts.

5 Row 5: *K2tog; rep from * across, end k1—7 (8, 8, 9) sts.

FINISHING

1 Cut yarn, leaving a tail long enough to sew the back seam. Pull tail through rem 7 (8, 8, 9) sts and tighten.

2 Sew the back seam, carefully running the seam 1 st in from edge on each side so that the rib looks even.

3 Weave in ends.

4 Lightly steam to block, pulling rib out a bit to flatten—but not so much that the hat is too stretched out.

These mittens are knit in the round on double-pointed needles. The bulky thick-and-thin yarn has a homey feel and knits up quickly. The size range covers the whole family.

Specifications

SIZES

XS (S, M, L)

Palm circumference: 6 (7¼, 8½, 9¾) inches

MATERIALS

2 (2, 3, 3) balls Dale of Norway *Ara* (100% wool, 55 yards/50g ball) in red #23063 or blue #15747

Set of four size 10½ (6.5mm) double-pointed needles

Small stitch holder

Tapestry needle

GAUGE

13 stitches and 21 rows to 4 inches over stockinette stitch on size 10½ (6.5mm) needles

CONTINUED ON NEXT PAGE

How to Make the Cozy Mittens

MITTEN CUFF

1. CO 20 (24, 28, 32) sts, dividing sts evenly over three dpns.
2. Place marker, join rnd, taking care not to twist sts, and work in K2, p2 rib every rnd for 2½ (3, 3½, 4) inches.
3. Change to St st (knit every rnd) and work for 2 rnds.

SHAPE THUMB GUSSET

Note: In this pattern you increase by using the bar increase (see page 48).

1. Next rnd: Inc 1 st in first st of rnd, inc 1 st in next st of rnd, k to end—22 (26, 30, 34) sts.
2. Knit 1 (1, 2, 2) rnds.
3. Next rnd: Inc 1 st in first st of rnd, k2, inc 1 st in next st of rnd, k to end—24 (28, 32, 36) sts.
4. Knit 1 (1, 2, 2) rnds.
5. Next rnd: Inc 1 st in first st of rnd, k4, inc 1 st in next st, k to end—26 (30, 34, 38) sts.
6. Knit 1 (2, 2, 2) rnds.
7. Next rnd: Inc 1 st in first st of rnd, k6, inc 1 st in next st, k to end—28 (32, 36, 40) sts.
8. Knit 1 (2, 2, 2) rnds.
9. Next rnd *(S, M, and L only)*: Inc 1 st in first st, k8, inc 1 st in next st—28 (34, 38, 42) sts.
10. All sizes: Knit 0 (1, 2, 2) rnds.
11. Next rnd: Slip first 8 (10, 10, 10) sts onto holder for thumb.

MITTEN BODY

1. Join rnd with rem 20 (24, 28, 32) sts for hand.
2. Knit every rnd until mitten is about 1 inch shorter than desired length.

SHAPE MITTEN TIP

1 Round 1: *K2, k2tog; rep from * to end of rnd—15 (18, 21, 24) sts.

2 Rounds 2 and 4: Knit.

3 Round 3: *K1, k2tog; rep from * to end of rnd—10 (12, 14, 16) sts.

4 Round 5: *K2tog; rep from * to end of rnd—5 (6, 7, 8) sts.

5 Final round: *K2tog; rep from * to end of rnd—3 (3, 4, 4) sts.

6 Cut yarn, leaving a 10-inch tail. Pull tail through rem sts, tighten, and fasten.

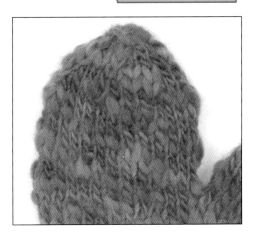

MITTEN THUMB

Note: *In this part of the pattern, you pick up stitches. For a refresher on how to do this, see page 154.*

1 Divide the 8 (10, 10, 10) sts from the holder evenly over three dpns. Pick up 2 sts from inside thumb on mitten hand—10 (12, 12, 12) sts.

2 Knit every rnd until thumb is about ¼ inch shorter than desired length.

3 K2tog across all sts next 2 rnds—3 sts.

4 Cut yarn, pull tail through the last 3 sts, and tighten.

FINISHING

1 Weave in ends, using end at cuff to secure the join of the first rnd, if necessary.

Note: *You can make a crochet mitten chain (see page 192) if desired. Simply crochet the chain a little shorter than the length of the arm span from wrist to wrist — arms held out to the sides. Sew ends to cuffs.*

Textured Pillow Cover

Making a hand-knit pillow cover is a great way to practice new texture, cable, or color stitch patterns because you don't have to worry about shaping. Be sure to get your gauge correct, though, so that your cover will fit properly onto your pillow form. This pillow cover is worked as two squares that are crocheted together.

Specifications

SIZE

12 inches x 12 inches

MATERIALS

4 balls Dale of Norway *Freestyle* (100% washable wool, 87 yards/50g ball) in orange #3227 (A) and 1 ball blue #5703 (B)

Note: *Yarn is used double throughout.*

Size 11 (8mm) needles

Tapestry needle

Size J (6mm) crochet hook

12 x 12 inch pillow form

GAUGE

12 stitches and 17 rows to 4 inches over Andalusian stitch on size 11 (8mm) needles *with yarn used double*

ANDALUSIAN STITCH (ODD NUMBER OF STS)

Row 1 (RS): Knit.

Row 2 (WS): Purl.

Row 3: K1, *p1, k1; rep from * to end.

Row 4: Purl.

Rep rows 1–4 for Andalusian stitch.

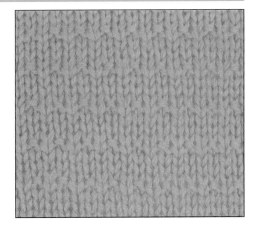

PILLOW COVER

1 CO 35 sts in double strand A.

2 Beg with row 1, work in Andalusian stitch pattern until piece measures 12 inches, ending with a WS row.

3 BO sts in patt. Cut yarn and pull tail through last st to secure.

4 Repeat steps 1–3 to create second side of cover.

FINISHING

1 Weave in ends.

2 Lightly steam on WS to block and reduce curling.

3 Hold squares together with WS facing each other. Work picot crochet (see page 195) in double strand B around three sides to join and embellish as follows: Working left to right, starting at corner and working through both thicknesses at the same time, work 1 single crochet (sc), *ch3, insert the crochet hook back into the same st and pull up loop, yo, and pull yarn through both loops on hook (this re-inserted chain is the picot); sc across next 3 sts; rep from * around three sides. Do not cut yarn or tie off end. Leave loop on holder.

4 Insert pillow form into cover, taking care not to let edging unravel and making sure the pillow form corners are tucked into the pillow cover corners.

5 Continue picot edging across fourth side to finish. Cut yarn and pull tail through last loop to secure. Thread the end into a tapestry needle and close edging to conceal end.

Bobble Bag

You will be very adept at making bobbles after completing this bag. It's another quick project, knitting up at 3 stitches per inch.

SIZE

9 inches x 9 inches, not including strap

MATERIALS

1 skein each Brown Sheep *Lamb's Pride Bulky* (85% wool/15% mohair, 125 yards/100g skein) in pink #M105 (A) and orange #M110 (B)

Size 10½ (6.5mm) needles

Tapestry needle

Size K (6.5mm) crochet hook

GAUGE

12 stitches and 18 rows to 4 inches over bobble stitch on size 10½ (6.5mm) needles

MB (MAKE BOBBLE)

Knit into front, back, front, back, and front (that's five times) of stitch. Then, without turning, pass fourth st over fifth and off, third st over fifth and off, second st over fifth and off, and first st over fifth and off.

BOBBLE STITCH (MULT OF 4 STS PLUS 3)

Row 1 (RS—bobble row): *K3, mb; repeat from * across row, end k3.

Rows 2, 4, and 6 (WS): Purl.

Rows 3 and 5: Knit.

Row 7 (bobble row): K1, mb, *k3, mb; rep from * across, end k1.

Rows 8, 10, and 12: Purl.

Rows 9 and 11: Knit.

Rep rows 1–12 for bobble stitch.

How to Make the Bobble Bag

BOBBLE BAG

1. CO 55 sts in A.
2. Work bobble st, starting at row 1, until piece measures approx 8 inches, ending with a row 1, 2, 7, or 8 of patt.
3. BO sts in patt. Cut yarn, leaving a tail long enough to sew seam.

FINISHING

1. Weave in ends, except the one for sewing the side seam.
2. Lightly steam on WS to block and reduce curling.
3. Fold piece in half vertically, with RS facing each other, and sew side seam. Lay piece flat and inside out, with seam at side, pin bottom edges together, and sew bottom seam.
4. Turn RS out and steam seams.
5. With crochet hook and B, and starting at side seam, work 2 rows of single crochet around top edge. Cut yarn, draw end through last loop, and weave in.
6. Make closure loop: With crochet hook and B, pick up a loop in middle of top edge at seam, work a 3-inch chain, and reattach where you began to form the loop. Secure and weave in ends. (Loop will fasten to the center front bobble at the top edge.)
7. Make strap: Using a 3½-yard strand of each color, twist the two strands together until quite firm. Then hold all 4 ends together and let the strands twist again by themselves to create a shorter quadruple-strand cord.
8. Sew each end of the cord to a corner of the bag.

15

Intermediate Knitting Projects

The knitting projects in this chapter include some techniques that are beyond the beginner level but are certainly not too difficult for you to handle. These projects offer a good opportunity to try your hand at cables, Fair Isle, textured stitches, and more involved shaping and finishing techniques. Certain procedures may be difficult to visualize from the instructions alone, but don't give up on a pattern before you've actually tried some of the techniques yourself.

Baby Booties

These booties are shaped by using a method similar to short-rowing (see pages 60–63). You may find it difficult to understand what is supposed to be happening by reading the instructions alone; but when you are doing what the directions tell you to, you will see how easily the booties take shape.

Specifications

SIZES

Newborn (3 mos., 6 mos., 9–12 mos.)

Instep: 2 (2¼, 2½, 2¾) inches

MATERIALS

2 balls elann.com's *Peruvian Collection Baby Cashmere* (60% baby alpaca/30% merino wool/10% cashmere, 109 yards/25g ball) in cream #100 (A) and a small amount of another yarn (B) for pompom and tie (sample used elann.com's *Peruvian Collection Pure Alpaca* in green #1256).

Note: *A double strand of this fingering weight yarn is used to make the booties.*

Pair of size 3 (3.25mm) needles

Two small stitch holders

Tapestry needle

Size D (3.25mm) crochet hook

Pompom maker

GAUGE

24 stitches and 32 rows to 4 inches over stockinette stitch on size 3 (3.25mm) needles *with yarn used double*

ANKLE

1 With size 3 needles and double strand of A, CO 27 (30, 33, 36) sts.

2 Work in garter stitch (knit every row) for 10 rows.

3 Work eyelet row: K3 (4, 4, 3), yo, k2tog, k3 (3, 4, 5), yo, k2tog, k8 (8, 10, 12), yo, k2tog, k3 (3, 4, 5), yo, k2tog, k2 (4, 3, 3).

4 Knit 3 rows. Cut yarn.

INSTEP

1 Slip first 9 (10, 11, 12) sts onto holder; join new double strand of yarn and k across next 9 (10, 11, 12) sts; slip last 9 (10, 11, 12) sts onto second holder.

2 Continuing on center 9 (10, 11, 12) instep sts only, beg from here with a purl row, work in St st (knit every row) until instep measures 2 (2¼, 2½, 2¾) inches from beg of St st—approx 17 (19, 21, 23) rows, ending with a WS row. Cut yarn.

3 Slip 9 (10, 11, 12) sts from first holder to same needle as instep sts. Join double strand of yarn and k across these 9 (10, 11, 12) sts; then pick up and k10 (11, 12, 13) sts along side edge of instep (with RS facing); k across the 9 (10, 11, 12) instep sts; pick up and k10 (11, 12, 13) sts along other side of instep (with RS facing), and then slip the rem 9 (10, 11, 12) sts from the second holder to the left needle and k to end—47 (52, 57, 62) sts.

4 Knit 11 (11, 13, 13) rows. Cut yarn.

SOLE

1 Next row (RS): Slip first 19 (21, 23, 25) sts from left needle to right needle. Join double strand of yarn and k9 (10, 11, 12) sts from left needle; turn.

2 Next row: K8 (9, 10, 11), k2tog tbl; turn.

3 Next row: K8 (9, 10, 11), k2tog; turn.

4 Rep last 2 rows (steps 2 and 3) until only the center 9 (10, 11, 12) sts rem.

5 Next row: k2tog; *k2tog, pass first st on right needle over second st on right needle and off; rep from *, k2tog and BO as you go, until 1 st rem. Cut yarn, leaving a long enough tail to sew back seam; pull tail through last st and secure.

CONTINUED ON NEXT PAGE

OTHER BOOTIE

Make a second bootie just like the first.

FINISHING

1. Turn bootie inside out and weave in ends, except the one that can be used to sew the back seam.

2. Turn back to RS and use B to work embroidery around edge of St st part of booties, if desired.

3. Sew back seam and weave in end.

4. Make two 1¼-inch tight pompoms in B (see page 180). Sew each pompom to back of bootie.

5. Make chain by cutting two 120-inch strands of B. Using both strands together, make a slip knot about 5 inches from one end and work a crochet chain (see page 192) until it is 18 inches long. Cut yarn, leaving a 5-inch tail.

6. Thread chain tails through a tapestry needle, bring ends back up into the chain to conceal them, and cut yarn.

7. Rep steps 5 and 6 for the other bootie.

8. Weave chains in and out of eyelets at ankle so that the ends come out toward the front. Tie each in a bow.

This is a very easy sweater. Knit in a simple stripe pattern, it has minimal shaping. Before you knit an adult size sweater, it's a good idea to try a baby sweater first. That way, you can learn how to construct an entire garment on a smaller scale, in much less time. Plus, a hand-knit sweater is one of the nicest gifts you can give to welcome a new baby into the world. The instructions here include sizes ranging from 6 months to 6 years, in case you don't have a baby to knit for.

Specifications

SIZES (See pattern schematic on next page.)

6 mos. (1–2 yrs., 3–4 yrs., 5–6 yrs.)

Back length: 11 (12½, 14, 15½) inches

Finished chest circumference: 22 (26, 29, 32) inches

Sleeve length: 6½ (8, 10, 12) inches

MATERIALS

2 (2, 2, 3) balls elann.com's *Peruvian Collection Highland Wool* (100% highland wool, 109 yards/50g ball) in orange #1004 (A), 1 (1, 1, 2) ball(s) in peridot #1477 (B), and 1 ball each in purple #1778 (C), yellow #7725 (D), and blue #2699 (E)

Size 6 (4mm) needles

Size 7 (4.5mm) needles

Size 6 (4mm) circular needle, at least 20 inches long, for working trim

Three stitch holders

Set of three size 6 (4mm) double-pointed needles for grafting shoulder seams

Row counter, if desired, to keep track of shaping rows on sleeves

Tapestry needle

Five ½- to ⅝-inch buttons

GAUGE

18 stitches and 24 rows to 4 inches over stockinette stitch on size 7 (4.5mm) needles

CONTINUED ON NEXT PAGE

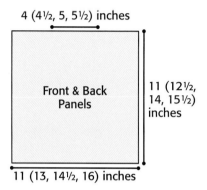

4 (4½, 5, 5½) inches

Front & Back
Panels

11 (12½,
14, 15½)
inches

11 (13, 14½, 16) inches

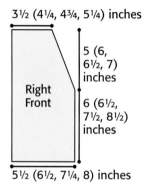

3½ (4¼, 4¾, 5¼) inches

Right
Front

5 (6,
6½, 7)
inches

6 (6½,
7½, 8½)
inches

5½ (6½, 7¼, 8) inches

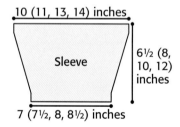

10 (11, 13, 14) inches

Sleeve

6½ (8,
10, 12)
inches

7 (7½, 8, 8½) inches

STRIPE PATTERN

Over stockinette stitch, work stripe patt as follows:

2 rows in B
2 rows in C
2 rows in D
2 rows in E
2 rows in A

Rep these 10 rows for stripe patt.

Note: *If you don't want to have to weave in so many ends, you can carry the yarns alternately up the side as you go (see page 118).*

SSK (LEFT-SLANTING) DECREASE

Slip first st as if to knit and then slip next st as if to knit. Insert left needle into front of slipped sts and knit them together.

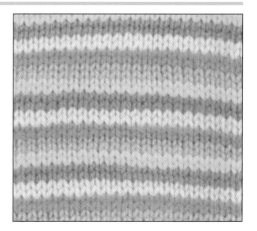

BACK

1. With size 6 needles and A, CO 50 (58, 65, 72) sts.

2. Knit 4 rows.

3. Change to size 7 needles and B, and, beg with a knit row, work in St st and stripe patt until back measures 11 (12½, 14½, 15½) inches from beg, ending with a WS row.

4. Put all sts onto a spare needle or holder for later.

CONTINUED ON NEXT PAGE

RIGHT FRONT

1 With size 6 needles and A, CO 25 (29, 33, 36) sts.

2 Knit 4 rows.

3 Change to size 7 needles and B, and, beg with a knit row, work in St st and stripe patt until front measures 6 (6½, 7½, 8½) inches from beg, ending with a WS row.

4 Shape neck: Ssk, k across to end.

5 Next row (WS): Purl.

6 Continue to dec 1 st at neck edge, as established, beg every RS row, maintaining stripe patt, until 16 (19, 21, 24) sts rem.

7 Continue without shaping until front measures same as back, ending with the same stripe.

8 Cut yarn, leaving a long tail, and put sts onto holder for later.

LEFT FRONT

Work as for right front, only shape neck *at the end of RS rows* by k2tog last 2 sts.

SLEEVES

1 With size 6 needles and A, CO 32 (34, 36, 38) sts.

2 Knit 4 rows.

3 Change to size 7 needles and work first 2 rows stripe patt.

Note: You may want to use a row counter to keep track of increase rows.

4 Next row (RS)—Begin sleeve shaping: Inc 1 st each end this row.

5 From here, inc 1 st each end every fourth row 4 (4, 7, 5) times, then every eighth row 2 (3, 3, 6) times—maintaining stripe patt—to 46 (50, 58, 62) sts.

6 Work without further shaping until sleeve measures 6½ (8, 10, 12) inches from beg, ending with a WS row. BO firmly but not tightly, using same color as final stripe.

7 Rep steps 1–6 to create second sleeve.

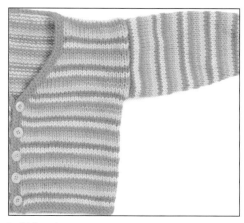

Left front

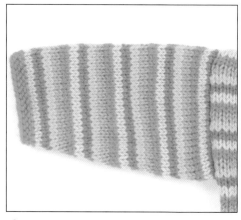

Sleeve

GRAFT SHOULDER SEAMS

Before working the trim, you need to join the shoulders. Use the three-needle bind-off method to graft shoulder seams, as described here. (See page 146 for more information.)

1. With RS together, place the 16 (19, 21, 24) sts from the left front shoulder onto a size 6 dpn, and do the same for the 16 (19, 21, 24) sts from the left back shoulder; then hold the needles parallel to one another.

2. Insert a third dpn into the first st on the first needle as if to knit, then into the first st on the second needle as if to knit, and k the 2 sts as 1.

3. Rep step 2; there should now be 2 sts on the right needle.

4. Pass the first st on the right needle over the second and off.

5. Continue to rep steps 3 and 4, knitting the corresponding sts of each shoulder together and binding off as you go, until 1 st rem on the right needle.

6. Cut yarn, pull it through the last st, and secure.

7. Rep steps 1–6 for the right shoulder.

WORK TRIM

1. With size 6 circular needle and A, beg at lower edge of right front, pick up and k30 (32, 37, 43) sts up to beg neck shaping, then pick up and k25 (30, 32, 35) sts up to shoulder seam, then k18 (20, 23, 24) sts from holder for back neck, then pick up and k25 (30, 32, 35) sts down left neck, then k30 (32, 37, 43) sts down to lower left edge—128 (144, 161, 180) sts.

2. Work buttonhole row (WS): K0 (2, 3, 1), k2tog, yo, *k5 (5, 6, 8), k2tog, yo; rep from * three more times, k to end.

3. Knit 2 rows.

4. BO sts knitwise.

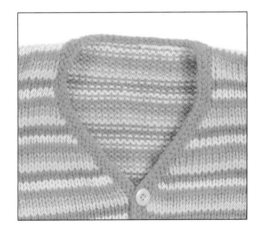

CONTINUED ON NEXT PAGE

FINISHING

1. Attach sleeves: With RS together and shoulder seams centered, pin sleeve caps to armholes. Backstitch in place (see page 141).

2. Weave in ends, except those that can be used to sew sleeve and side seams later.

3. Lightly steam entire sweater on WS, including seams, to block.

4. Sew side and sleeve seams. (See pages 140–143 for more information.)

5. Lightly steam again.

6. Sew buttons opposite buttonholes with matching yarn or thread.

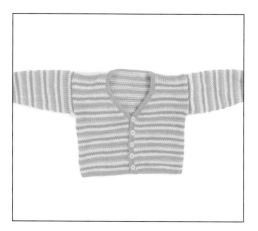

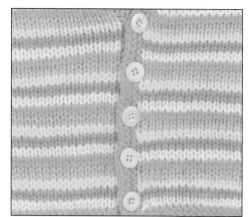

Mini Tote Bag

You can make any number of purses and bags like this one by simply making rectangles in various stitch patterns, sewing them together, and attaching handles. This particular bag is worked in stitch patterns that lie flat. The pieces are then simply whipstitched together.

Specifications

SIZE

8½ inches wide x 4 inches deep x 5¼ inches high, not including handles

MATERIALS

1 ball each Muench Yarns/GGH *Via Mala* (100% merino wool, 73 yards/50g ball) in blue-green #42 (A), brown #20 (B), and gold #34 (C)

Size 11 (8mm) needles

Size 10 (6mm) needles

Tapestry needle

Size J (6mm) crochet hook

One 1-inch button to match C

GAUGE

12 stitches and 20 rows over stockinette stitch on size 10 (6mm) needles

CONTINUED ON NEXT PAGE

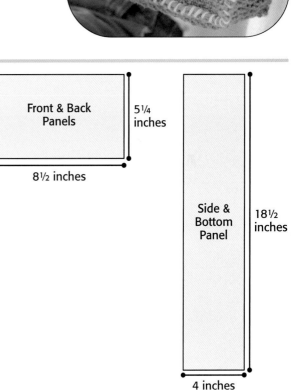

Front & Back Panels

5¼ inches

8½ inches

Side & Bottom Panel

18½ inches

4 inches

Pattern Stitches

LINEN STITCH (EVEN NUMBER OF STS)

Row 1 (RS): *K1, slip 1 wyif; rep from * to last 2 sts, end k2.

Row 2 (WS): *P1, slip 1 wyib; rep from * to last 2 sts, end p2.

Rep rows 1 and 2 for linen stitch.

SMALL BASKETWEAVE STITCH (MULT OF 4 STS PLUS 3)

Rows 1 and 3 (RS): Knit.

Row 2 (WS): *K3, p1; rep from * to last 3 sts, end k3.

Row 4: K1, *p1, k3; rep from * to last 2 sts, end p1, k1.

Rep rows 1–4 for small basketweave stitch.

RIBBING STITCH (ODD NUMBER OF STS)

Row 1 (WS): P1, *k1, p1; rep from * to end.

Row 2 (RS): K1, *p1, k1; rep from * to end.

Rep rows 1 and 2 for ribbing stitch.

How to Make the Mini Tote Bag

FRONT PANEL

1 With size 11 needles and A, CO 32 sts.

2 Work in linen st until piece measures 5¼ inches from beg, ending with a WS row.

3 Slip sts onto size 10 needle and use second size 10 needle to BO sts in patt.

BACK PANEL

Make a back panel just like the front.

SIDE/BOTTOM PANEL

1 With size 10 needles and B, CO 15 sts.

2 Work in small basketweave st until piece measures 18½ inches (or the same length as the sum of the bottom edge plus both sides of one of the linen st panels), ending with a RS row.

3 BO sts in patt.

FINISHING

1. Weave in ends.
2. Block pieces, if desired.
3. Whipstitch (see page 188) the panels together in C, as shown. Reinforce the top corners with a few extra stitches.
4. Sew button to center of top edge of front panel, using a few separated plies of B.

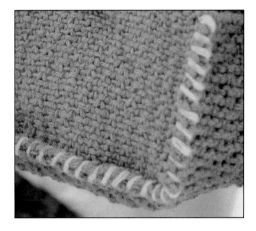

BUTTON LOOP

1. Use B to make crochet chain (see page 192) that is 3¼ inches long, leaving tails on each end long enough to sew loop to top edge of back panel.
2. Sew ends of chain at center of back panel, about 1 inch apart. Secure and weave in ends.

HANDLES

1. Using size 10 needles and C, pick up and k5 sts, starting about 1½ inches in from side edge, leaving a 10-inch tail. Turn.
2. Work in ribbing st, beg with row 1 (WS), and continue until handle measures 8½–9½ inches, or desired length.
3. BO sts in patt, leaving a 15-inch tail.
4. Sew bound-off end of handle to other end of panel, as shown.
5. Rep steps 1–4 for second handle.
6. Use tails to wrap yarn around seam as shown at far right.

Turtleneck Sweater

This is a good basic sweater for both men and women. With this project you learn how to shape shoulders and pick up stitches to knit on a collar, and you learn basic sweater construction. There is no armhole shaping, so attaching the sleeves is very simple. You can try several variations: If you don't want a turtleneck, you can make the sweater a crewneck by knitting the collar for only a couple inches; or if you want a cropped style, you can work the body for fewer inches.

Specifications

SIZES

Women's S (Women's M, Women's L, Men's S, Men's M, Men's L)

Back length: 24 (24½, 25, 26, 26½, 27) inches

Finished chest circumference: 42 (44, 46, 48, 50, 52) inches

Sleeve length: 18 (18½, 19, 19½, 20, 20½) inches

MATERIALS

10 (10, 11, 11, 12, 12) hanks Cascade Yarns *109* (100% Peruvian highland wool, 109 yards/100g hank) in cream #8010

Size 9 (5.5mm) needles for ribbing

Size 9 (5.5mm) circular needle, at least 16 inches long, for collar

Size 10½ (6.5mm) needles

Two large stitch holders

Row counter, if desired, to keep track of shaping rows on sleeves

Tapestry needle

GAUGE

13 stitches and 22 rows over stockinette stitch on size 10½ (6.5mm) needles

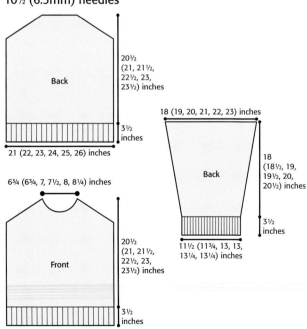

Back

20½ (21, 21½, 22½, 23, 23½) inches

3½ inches

21 (22, 23, 24, 25, 26) inches

6¾ (6¾, 7, 7½, 8, 8¼) inches

Front

20½ (21, 21½, 22½, 23, 23½) inches

3½ inches

18 (19, 20, 21, 22, 23) inches

Back

18 (18½, 19, 19½, 20, 20½) inches

3½ inches

11½ (11¾, 13, 13, 13¼, 13¼) inches

RIBBING STITCH

When the number of sts is a multiple of 5 sts plus 2, work ribbing as follows:

Row 1 (RS): P2, *k3, p2; rep from * to end.

Row 2 (WS): K2, *p3, k2; rep from * to end.

Rep rows 1 and 2 for ribbing stitch.

When the number of sts is a multiple of 5 sts plus 3, work ribbing as follows:

Row 1 (RS): K3, *p2, k3; rep from * to end.

Row 2 (WS): P3, *k2, p3; rep from * to end.

Rep rows 1 and 2 for ribbing stich.

How to Make the Turtleneck Sweater

BACK

① With size 9 needles, CO 68 (72, 77, 78, 82, 87) sts.

② Work ribbing as instructed for your st count for 3½ inches, ending with a WS row.

③ Change to size 10½ needles and work in St st until back measures 24 (24½, 25, 26, 26½, 27) inches from beg, ending with a WS row.

④ Shape shoulders: BO 11 (12, 13, 13, 14, 15) sts beg next 2 rows, then 11 (12, 13, 13, 13, 14) beg foll 2 rows—24 (24, 25, 26, 28, 29) sts.

⑤ Place rem sts on a holder or spare needle.

FRONT

① Work steps 1–3 as for back until front measures 21½ (22, 22½, 23½, 24, 24) inches from beg, ending with a WS row.

② Shape neck: K across first 28 (30, 32, 32, 33, 35) sts. Turn and work on these sts only (put rem sts on spare circular needle).

③ Working in St st, dec 1 st at neck edge every row, until 22 (24, 26, 26, 27, 29) sts rem.

④ Work until left side of front measures 24 (24½, 25, 26, 26½, 27) inches from beg, ending with a WS row.

⑤ Begin left shoulder shaping: BO 11 (12, 13, 13, 14, 15) sts beg this row, k to end.

⑥ Next row (WS): Purl.

CONTINUED ON NEXT PAGE

7. Next row: BO rem 11 (12, 13, 13, 13, 14) sts.

8. Cut yarn, leaving a 15-inch tail to sew shoulder seam later.

9. Slip center 12 (12, 13, 14, 16, 17) sts onto holder for neck. Slip rem 28 (30, 32, 32, 33, 35) sts back onto needle, ready to begin a RS row.

10. Join yarn and rep steps 3 and 4 but end with a RS row.

11. Next row—Begin right shoulder shaping: BO 11 (12, 13, 13, 14, 15) sts beg this row, p to end.

12. Next row (RS): Knit.

13. Last row: BO rem 11 (12, 13, 13, 13, 14) sts.

14. Cut yarn, leaving a 15-inch tail to sew shoulder seam later.

SLEEVES

1. With size 9 (5.5mm) needles, CO 37 (38, 42, 42, 43, 43) sts.

2. Work ribbing as instructed for your st count for 3½ inches, ending with a WS row.

   Note: *You may want to use a row counter to keep track of increase rows.*

3. Next row—Begin sleeve shaping: Change to size 10½ needles, and, working in St st, inc 1 st each end first row and every eighth row 8 (6, 10, 5, 4, 0) times, then every sixth row 2 (5, 0, 7, 9, 15) times—59 (62, 64, 68, 71, 75) sts.

4. Continue without further shaping until sleeve measures 18 (18½, 19, 19½, 20, 20½) inches from beg, ending with a WS row.

5. BO sts knitwise.

6. Rep steps 1–5 to complete second sleeve.

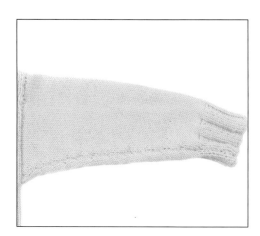

FINISHING

1. Weave in ends, except those that can be used to sew seams.

2. Block pieces to measurements shown on page 238.

3. Sew left shoulder seam.

4. Work turtleneck: Join yarn and use size 9 circular needle to k11 (11, 12, 12, 13, 13) sts from holder for back neck, k2tog, k11 (11, 11, 12, 13, 14) sts from holder for back neck; pick up and k14 (14, 15, 14, 15, 16) sts down left front neck shaping, k12 (12, 13, 14, 16, 17) sts from holder for front neck; pick up and k14 (14, 15, 15, 15, 16) sts up right front neck—63 (63, 67, 68, 73, 77) sts.

5. Work ribbing as instructed for your st count until collar measures 7 (7, 7½, 7½, 8, 8) inches.

6. BO sts loosely in patt.

7. Sew right shoulder seam and collar seam.

8. Center sleeves on shoulder seams with RS together and sew sleeves onto sweater.

9. Lightly steam seams.

10. Sew side and sleeve seams.

11. Weave in rem ends.

12. Steam entire sweater, including seams, again.

Child's Raglan Sweater with Fair Isle Details

This project familiarizes you with raglan shaping and Fair Isle knitting. The Fair Isle sections are only a few rows long, so this pattern is not too difficult. Remember to include the Fair Isle pattern when working your gauge swatch. If you get a slightly tighter gauge on the Fair Isle section, try working that part on needles one size larger. If you want to make a very easy version of this sweater, you can eliminate the Fair Isle patterns at the hem and cuffs.

Specifications

SIZES (See pattern schematic on next page.)

2 (4, 6, 8) years

Back length: 14 (16¼, 18½, 21) inches

Finished chest circumference: 26 (29½, 33, 37) inches

Sleeve length: 7½ (8½, 10½, 11½) inches

MATERIALS

2 (3, 4, 4) hanks S.R. Kertzer *Super 3* (100% cotton, 186 yards/125g hank) in linen #3203 (A), and 1 hank each in alpine sky blue #3801 (B), espresso #3334 (C), and cream (D)

Size 8 (5mm) needles

Size 8 (5mm) circular needle, 20 inches long

Four stitch holders

Row counter, if desired, to keep track of shaping rows on sleeves

Tapestry needle

GAUGE

18 stitches and 22 rows to 4 inches over stockinette stitch on size 8 (5mm) needles

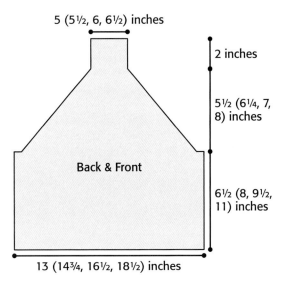

5 (5½, 6, 6½) inches

2 inches

5½ (6¼, 7, 8) inches

Back & Front

6½ (8, 9½, 11) inches

13 (14¾, 16½, 18½) inches

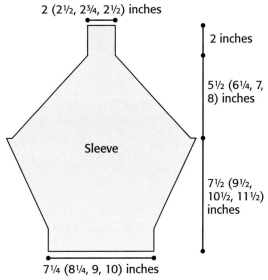

2 (2½, 2¾, 2½) inches

2 inches

5½ (6¼, 7, 8) inches

Sleeve

7½ (9½, 10½, 11½) inches

7¼ (8¼, 9, 10) inches

CONTINUED ON NEXT PAGE

Pattern Stitch and Charts

SSK (LEFT-SLANTING) DECREASE

Slip first st as if to knit and then slip next st as if to knit. Insert left needle into front of slipped sts and knit them together.

FAIR ISLE COLOR CHARTS

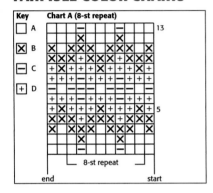

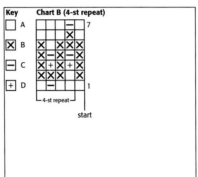

How to Make the Child's Raglan Sweater

BACK

1. Using B and long-tail CO method (see pages 16–17), CO 59 (67, 75, 83) sts.

2. Change to A and, beg with a purl row, work 7 (9, 11, 13) rows in St st.

3. Next row (RS): Starting with row 1 of chart A, work through all 13 rows of color patt, beg and ending rows where indicated on chart.

4. Continue working St st in only A until piece measures 6½ (8, 9½, 11) inches from beg, ending with a WS row.

5. Shape raglan armhole: BO 3 (4, 5, 5) sts beg next 2 rows.

6. Next row (RS): K3, ssk, k across to last 5 sts, k2tog, k3.

7. Next row: Purl.

8. Rep these last 2 rows (steps 6 and 7) until 23 (25, 27, 29) sts rem.

9. Work another 2 inches (about 12 rows) without shaping, ending with a WS row. Place sts on holder.

FRONT

Complete as for back, leaving sts on holder for later.

SLEEVES

1. Using B and long-tail CO method, CO 33 (37, 41, 45) sts.

2. Change to A and, beg with a purl row, work 5 (5, 7, 7) rows St st.

3. Next row (RS): Starting with row 1 of chart B, work through all 7 rows of color patt, beg rows where indicated on chart.

4. Next row: Change back to only A and purl 1 row.

   Note: You may want to use a row counter to keep track of increase rows.

5. Next row–Begin sleeve shaping: Using A, inc 1 st each end this row, then inc 1 st each end every fourth row 5 (7, 9, 9) times—45 (53, 61, 65) sts.

6. Work without further shaping until sleeve measures 7½ (9½, 10½, 11½) inches from beg, ending with a WS row.

7. Shape sleeve cap: BO 3 (4, 5, 5) sts beg next 2 rows.

8. Next row (RS): K3, ssk, k across to last 5 sts, k2tog, k3.

9. Next: Purl.

10. Rep these last 2 rows (steps 8 and 9) until 9 (11, 13, 11) sts rem.

11. Work another 2 inches (about 12 rows) without shaping, ending with a WS row. Place sts on holder.

12. Rep steps 1–11 to complete second sleeve.

FINISHING

1. Weave in ends, except those that can be used to sew seams.

2. Sew all raglan seams, except the one for the right back raglan seam.

3. Slip sts from back neck, right sleeve, front neck, and left sleeve holders onto size 8 circular needle. Join yarn B and k22 (24, 26, 28) sts, k2tog, k7 (9, 11, 9) sts, k2tog, k21 (23, 25, 27) sts, k2tog, k8 (10, 12, 10) sts.

4. BO sts purlwise.

5. Steam entire sweater, including seams.

6. Sew rem raglan seam, joining neck trim.

7. Sew side and sleeve seams.

8. Steam sweater, including seams, again.

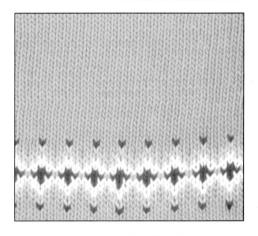

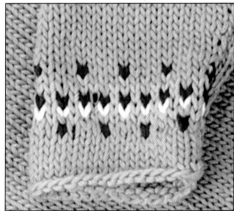

This sweater looks more complicated than it actually is. There is no cable work on the back, and the cluster rib, while it does employ a cable needle, does not involve actually moving stitches around. This pattern has set-in sleeves, so the sleeve cap shaping matches the armhole shaping.

SIZES (See pattern schematic on next page.)

S (M, L)

Back length: 18 (18½, 19) inches

Finished chest circumference: 35½ (38, 40) inches

Sleeve length: 18½ (19, 19½) inches

MATERIALS

6 (7, 7) hanks Plymouth Yarns *Baby Alpaca Grande* (100% baby alpaca, 110 yards/100g hank) in blue #3317

Size 10 (6mm) needles

Set of three size 9 (5.5mm) double-pointed needles for grafting shoulder seams

Row counter, if desired, to keep track of cable pattern and shaping rows on sleeves

Cable needle (cn)

Four stitch holders

Size J (6mm) crochet hook for trim

Tapestry needle

One 1-inch toggle button

GAUGE

14 stitches and 18 rows to 4 inches over stockinette stitch on size 10 (6mm) needles

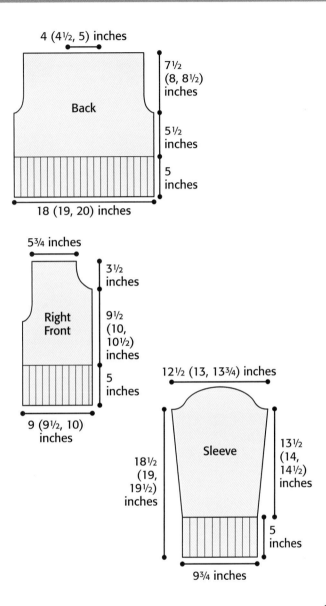

4 (4½, 5) inches

7½ (8, 8½) inches

Back

5½ inches

5 inches

18 (19, 20) inches

5¾ inches

3½ inches

Right Front

9½ (10, 10½) inches

5 inches

9 (9½, 10) inches

12½ (13, 13¾) inches

18½ (19, 19½) inches

Sleeve

13½ (14, 14½) inches

5 inches

9¾ inches

CONTINUED ON NEXT PAGE

Pattern Stitches

SSK (LEFT-SLANTING) DECREASE

Slip first st as if to knit and then slip next st as if to knit. Insert left needle into front of slipped sts and knit them together.

LEFT FRONT RIBBING STITCH (ODD NUMBER OF STS)

Row 1 (RS): P1 (2, 3), k2, *p2, k2; rep from * to last 0 (1, 2) sts, end p0 (1, 2).

Row 2 (WS): K0 (1, 2), p2, *k2, p2; rep from * to last 1 (2, 3) sts, end k1 (2, 3).

Rep rows 1 and 2 for left front ribbing.

RIGHT FRONT RIBBING STITCH (ODD NUMBER OF STS)

Row 1 (RS): P0 (1, 2), k2, *p2, k2; rep from * to last 1 (2, 3) sts, end p1 (2, 3).

Row 2 (WS): K1 (2, 3), p2, *k2, p2; rep from * to last 0 (1, 2) sts, end k0 (1, 2).

Rep rows 1 and 2 for right front ribbing.

CLUSTER RIB CABLE PANEL (14 STS)

Rows 1, 5, 7, 9, 11, 13, 15 (RS): P2, *k2, p2; rep from * twice.

Row 2 and all other WS rows: K2, *p2, k2; rep from * twice.

Row 3 (cable row): P2, k2, *p2, k2; rep from * once; slip the last 10 sts worked from the right needle onto cn and wrap working yarn around these 10 sts, counterclockwise, three times; slip the wrapped stitches back to the right needle; p2.

Row 16: Rep row 2.

Rep rows 1–16 for cluster rib cable.

How to Make the Women's Cropped Cardigan

BACK

1. With size 10 needles, CO 62 (66, 70) sts.
2. Row 1 (RS)—Work 2 x 2 ribbing: K2, *p2, k2; rep from * to end.
3. Row 2: P2, *k2, p2; rep from * to end.
4. Rep rows 1 and 2 until piece measures 5 inches, ending with a WS row.
5. Next row (RS): Beg with a knit row, work in St st until back measures 10½ inches, ending with a WS row.
6. Shape armhole: BO 2 sts beg next 2 rows.
7. Next row (RS): K1, ssk, k to last 3 sts, k2tog, k1.
8. Next row: Purl.
9. Rep last 2 rows (steps 7 and 8) 1 (2, 3) more time(s)—54 (56, 58) sts.
10. Continue without further shaping until back measures 17 (17½, 18) inches from beg, ending with a RS row. The armhole should measure 6½ (7, 7½) inches.

11. Next row (WS)—Beg neck shaping: P22, BO 10 (12, 14) sts, p22 sts.

12. Next row: Working on right shoulder sts only, k across to last 2 sts, k2tog.

13. Next row: Purl.

14. Next row: Rep previous RS row (step 12)—20 sts.

15. Work this shoulder without further shaping until piece measures 18 (18½, 19) inches from beg, ending with a RS row.

16. Cut yarn, leaving a tail long enough to knit shoulder seam, and put sts on holder.

17. Working on left shoulder sts, join yarn, and, beg with a RS row, ssk, k to end.

18. Next row (WS): Purl.

19. Ssk, k to end—20 sts.

20. Rep steps 15 and 16 to finish left shoulder, leaving sts on holder for later.

LEFT FRONT

Left front

1. With size 10 needles, CO 31 (33, 35) sts.

2. Work in left front ribbing st, beg with row 1 (RS), until front measures 5 inches from beg, ending with a WS row.

    Note: You may want to use a row counter to keep track of cluster rib cable pattern rows.

3. Next row (RS—Begin cluster rib cable): K7 (8, 9) sts, work row 1 of cluster rib cable panel across next 14 sts, k10 (11, 12) sts.

4. Next row: P10 (11, 12) sts, work row 2 of cluster rib cable panel over next 14 sts, p7 (8, 9) sts.

5. Continue working in this manner, with cluster rib cable panel positioned as established, until piece measures 10½ inches from beg, ending with a WS row.

6. Shape armhole: BO 2 sts beg next row.

7. Next row (WS): Work across row in patt.

8. Next row: K1, ssk, patt to end.

9. Rep last 2 rows (steps 7 and 8) until 27 (28, 29) sts rem.

10. Continue working without shaping until piece measures 14½ (15, 15½) inches from beg, ending with a RS row.

11. Shape neck (WS): BO 3 sts beg next row, then dec 1 st at neck edge every RS row (by working across to last 3 sts, k2tog, k1) until 20 sts rem.

12. Work to same length as back. Put sts on holder.

CONTINUED ON NEXT PAGE

RIGHT FRONT

1 With size 10 needles, CO 31 (33, 35) sts.

2 Work in right front ribbing st, beg with row 1 (RS), until front measures 5 inches from beg, ending with a WS row.

Note: You may want to use a row counter to keep track of cluster rib cable pattern rows.

3 Next row (RS–Begin cluster rib cable): K10 (11, 12) sts, work row 1 of cluster rib cable panel across next 14 sts, k7 (8, 9) sts.

4 Next row: P7 (8, 9) sts, work row 2 of cluster rib cable panel across next 14 sts, p10 (11, 12) sts.

5 Continue working in this manner, with cluster rib cable panel positioned as established, until piece measures 10½ inches from beg, ending with a RS row.

6 Shape armhole: BO 2 sts beg next row, then dec 1 st at armhole edge every RS row (by working across row to last 3 sts, k2tog, k1) until 27 (28, 29) sts rem.

Right front

7 Continue working without shaping until piece measures 14½ (15, 15½) inches from beg, ending with a WS row.

8 Shape neck (RS): BO 3 sts beg next row, then dec 1 st at neck edge every RS row (by k1, ssk, patt to end) until 20 sts rem.

9 Work to same length as back. Put sts on holder.

SLEEVES

1 With size 10 needles, CO 34 sts.

2 Work 2 x 2 ribbing as for back until piece measures 5 inches from beg, ending with a WS row.

Note: You may want to use a row counter to keep track of cluster cable pattern and sleeve increase rows.

3 Next row (RS–Begin cluster rib cable): K10 sts, work row 1 of cluster rib cable panel across next 14 sts, k to end.

4 Next row: P10 sts, work row 2 of cluster rib panel across next 14 sts, p to end.

5 Continue working in this manner, with cluster rib panel positioned as established.

AT THE SAME TIME, shape sleeve: Inc 1 st each end this row, then every 8th row 0 (2, 4) times, then every 12th row 4 (3, 2) times–44 (46, 48) sts. Work without further shaping until sleeve measures 18½ (19, 19½) inches from beg, ending with a WS row.

6 Shape sleeve cap: BO 2 sts beg next 2 rows, then dec 1 st each end every RS row 6 (7, 8) times (by k1, ssk, k across to last 3 sts, k2tog, k1) until 28 sts rem.

7 BO 2 sts beg next 4 rows–20 sts.

8 BO sts in patt.

9 Rep steps 1–8 to complete second sleeve.

FINISHING

For this sweater, you use the three-needle bind-off method to graft shoulder seams as described in steps 2–9. (See page 146 for more information.)

1 Block all pieces to measurements shown on page 247.

2 Place the 20 sts from the left front onto a size 9 dpn, and do the same for the 20 sts from the back left shoulder; then hold the needles parallel to each other, with RS together.

3 Insert a third dpn into the first st on the first needle as if to knit, then into the first st on the second needle as if to knit, and knit the 2 sts as 1.

4 Rep step 3; there should now be 2 sts on the right needle.

5 Pass the first st on the right needle over the second and off.

6 K the next 2 sts on the parallel dpn together.

7 Rep steps 5 and 6, knitting the corresponding sts of each shoulder together and binding off as you go, until 1 st rem on the right needle.

8 Cut yarn, pull through last st, and secure.

9 Rep steps 2–8 for the right shoulder seam.

10 With RS together, line up sleeve cap shaping with armhole shaping and pin in place. Sew sleeve to cardigan.

11 Weave in ends, except those that can be used to sew seams.

12 Lightly steam seams.

13 Place marker for button on left front ½ inch down from beg neck shaping.

14 Beg at lower edge of right front, use crochet hook to single crochet (see page 194) 1 row up right front, around neck, and back down left front to edge.

15 Work another single crochet row up left front and around neck to the point on the right front opposite the left-side marker. Ch1, then reinsert hook after skipping 1 single crochet stitch, about ¼ inch down from last single crochet, so that the chain button loop lies flush along the vertical front edge. Then single crochet down until you reach the end of the right front. Cut yarn, pull up through last loop, and secure.

16 Weave in rem ends. Sew side and sleeve seams.

17 Lightly steam entire sweater, including seams and crochet trim, again.

18 Sew button opposite button loop.

I would prefer to have buttons running all the way down the front, instead of just one button at the neck. How can I do that?

To add more buttons and buttonholes to this pattern, work through step 12, above. Then, for step 13, place markers for more buttons along the left front edge: Place one marker 1 inch up from the bottom, one ½ inch down from beg neck shaping, and five more, evenly spaced, between those two. Work step 14. Work step 15 through to the completion of the first button loop, and then work six more button loops in the same manner, opposite the markers on the left. Finish as instructed above, except sew seven buttons opposite the button loops.

Cable Knit Headband

This is a small project that is packed with lessons for you: It has a cable, stitches in the cable are wrapped in a contrast color, and it has a picot-edged hem. This could be worked very successfully in wool for a winter headband.

SIZES

XS (S, M, L)

15½ (16¾, 19, 20) inches

MATERIALS

1 skein each Dale of Norway *Svale* (50% cotton/10% silk/40% viscose, 114 yards/50g skein) in lime green #9425 (A) and yellow #2005 (B)

Size 5 (3.75mm) needles

Cable needle (cn)

Tapestry needle

GAUGE

22 stitches and 28 rows to 4 inches over stockinette stitch on size 5 (3.75mm) needles

Pattern Stitches

T2F STITCH

Slip next st onto cn and hold at front. P next st from left needle and then k st from cn.

T2B STITCH

Slip next st onto cn and hold at back. K next st from left needle and then p st from cn.

CABLE PANEL (6 STS)

Row 1 (WS): P1, k4, p1.

Row 2 (RS): T2f, p2, t2b.

Row 3 and all foll WS rows: K the k sts and p the p sts.

Row 4: P1, t2f, t2b, p1.

Row 6: P2, k2; sl last 2 sts worked onto cn and wrap yarn B around these 2 sts six times, counterclockwise; sl the two wrapped sts back to the right needle; p2.

Row 8: P1, t2b, t2f, p1.

Row 10: T2b, p2, t2f.

How to Make the Cable Knit Headband

HEADBAND

1. With B, CO 86 (92, 104, 110) sts. Work 8 rows St st.
2. Next row (RS—Work eyelet): K1, *k2tog, yo; rep from * to last st, end k1.
3. Next row: Purl.
4. Changing to A and, beg with a knit row, work 3 rows St st.
5. Next row (WS): P1, *row 1 cable; rep from * 14 (15, 17, 18) times across row, end p1.
6. Next row: K1, *row 2 cable; rep from * 14 (15, 17, 18) times across row, end k1.
7. Cont working cable rep as set, with 1 extra st each end, through last row (row 10) of cable panel.
8. Next row (WS): Beg with a purl row, work 2 rows St st. Change to B and p 1 row.
9. Next row: Rep step 2.
10. Beg with a purl row, work 7 rows St st.
11. BO sts knitwise.

FINISHING

1. Weave in ends.
2. Fold headband in half with RS together and backstitch (see page 141) short ends together to form band.
3. Fold in edges with WS together at eyelet rows to form picot edges at both sides and stitch cast-on edge and bound-off edge tog all around.
4. Lightly steam. Tack at intervals with needle and yarn or thread through both thicknesses to secure.

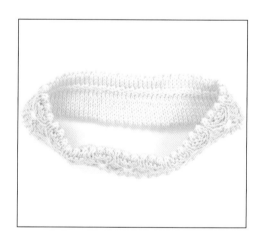

chapter **16**

Pick Up Your Needles and . . .

Now that you are a dedicated knitter, you can take your hobby in new directions. You may want to put your talents to a good cause by knitting preemie hats for your local hospital. Or you could join or start a knitting group, so that you can share tips, ideas, and pleasant hours with other knitters. You might even want to pass along your new knowledge of knitting by teaching a child (of any age) to knit.

When you're knitting something for someone, it's like you're weaving your love and good wishes into every stitch. You can do this for people you don't know by knitting for charity. Whether you're knitting hats, booties, and blankets for your local hospital, or comfortable throws for shut-ins, you will find tremendous satisfaction in donating your hand-knits to a worthy cause. Listed here are just a few organizations that accept donations.

CAPS FOR KIDS

Caps for Kids collects hand-knit caps and scarves for babies and children undergoing cancer treatment and treatment for other life-threatening illnesses. Many yarn shops collect items for Caps for Kids. To find a registered store near you, call the Craft Yarn Council at 800-662-9999, or visit the Caps for Kids Web site, at www.capsforkids.com. If you can't find a store near you that accepts donations, you can send your donations to:

Caps for Kids
c/o Bonnie Lawless
20112 Echo Blue Drive
Penn Valley, CA 95946-9422

WARM UP AMERICA

You can knit a 7 x 9-inch rectangle and donate it to Warm Up America. Warm Up America collects these hand-knit or crocheted rectangles and assembles them into afghans, which it

then donates to the homeless, disaster victims, and shelters for battered women. These afghans have brought warmth and comfort to many people in need. For more information, visit www.warmupamerica.com.

PROJECT LINUS

Project Linus has provided more than a million handmade blankets to children who are ill, traumatized, or in some other way in need of a security blanket. The organization accepts new, washable handmade blankets—either quilted, sewn, crocheted, or knit. To find free blanket patterns and specifications, and to find your local Project Linus chapter, visit www.projectlinus.org.

WARMING FAMILIES

Warming Families distributes new blankets, clothing, and other warm items to homeless and displaced people. You can get more information about where to send donations at www.warmingfamilies.org.

OTHER CHARITIES

You can contact your town or city's local shelters, hospitals, day-care centers, and nursing homes to see if they are in need of hand-knit donations. Here are a few other charity knitting Web sites:

www.chemocaps.com
www.binkypatrol.com
www.afghansforafghans.com
www.critterknitters.org

You can also visit the following Web sites to find charities looking for donations of hand-knits:

www.woolworks.org/charity.html
www.knitting.about.com/od/charityprojects

Starting a Knitting Group

It's fun to share your love of knitting with others. A perfect way to do this is to start or join a knitting group. All kinds of knitting groups have started up across the country over the past few years, in a wide variety of venues.

THE KNITTING/BOOK GROUP

Why not combine your love of reading with your love of knitting? Get a group of knitter/readers together, and when you reach a consensus about what work of literature you would like to read and discuss together, set a monthly schedule. You can get together at each other's homes on a revolving basis and discuss that month's book while working your needles.

THE CAFÉ KNITTING GROUP

Many knitters have started knitting groups that meet once a week at a local café. Sharing knitting tips and conversation over a cappuccino is a delightful way to pass an hour on a Sunday afternoon. Café proprietors often welcome the business, as long as everyone purchases something from the shop.

THE CHILDREN'S AND TEENS' KNITTING GROUP

A wonderful outcome of knitting's growth in popularity has been the formation of after-school knitting groups. Children of all ages are taking up knitting. It's a great opportunity for them to create, relax, do a little bit of simple math, get a little hand–eye coordination practice, and tune their fine motor skills. Check at your local schools to see if a knitting group exists, and, if not, why not start one?

THE GOURMET KNITTING GROUP

Another fun group is the gourmet knitting group. Many knitters are excellent cooks who love to share recipes as well as knitting patterns. Why not get together a small group and have a monthly potluck? Brunch is a good meal that provides the opportunity to test all kinds of recipes—both savory and sweet—and also leaves the afternoon open for knitting.

THE MOVIE NIGHT KNITTING GROUP

Many knitters do the bulk of their knitting while watching movies on TV. Getting together a group of knitters to do just that is even more fun. Have a little show-and-tell about knitting projects before and after the movie. And don't forget the popcorn.

Teaching a Child to Knit

You will find that when your friends and family members see you knitting, they will want to learn, too. Here are some guidelines to help you pass on your hobby. They are geared toward children but of course can be used to teach adults as well.

BEFORE YOU BEGIN

Before you begin to teach someone to knit, it's a good idea to collect the supplies you need and have a few small sample projects already made to show your student. Some good children's projects are small bags, narrow scarves, beanbags, doll scarves and blankets, and hand puppets. There are also short needles available that are well-suited to small hands. Remember that children will lose interest in a long and complicated demonstration or in a first project that takes a long time to complete. Make it fun and fast, and use fat yarn so that the child can get excited and have the satisfaction of finishing something quickly.

FINGER KNITTING

Very young children have difficulty handling two knitting needles, and trying to teach them is likely to be frustrating and disappointing for both of you. The best thing for little ones

who want to "knit" along with you is to try finger knitting. Finger knitting involves simply making a chain (see page 192) with the fingers instead of a crochet hook. These chains can be used for all kinds of things: hair ribbons, bracelets, belts, or leashes for stuffed animals. Try using a double strand of two different colors to make the chains even more interesting.

THE KNITTING NODDY

The next step after finger knitting is using a knitting noddy. You hold a knitting noddy in one hand while you use your other hand to work the yarn around the points. The result is a knitted tube that you can use for belts, hair ties, headbands, play rope, or whatever a child's imagination can conjure up.

THE RHYME

You can teach children under 7 or 8 to knit with two needles, but you will generally have more success with children 8 years or older. It also helps if the child knows how to read, so that she or he can follow a simple pattern, if desired. When you are teaching children to knit on two needles, you can break down the steps by reciting the following rhyme:

> *In through the front door* (sticking the right needle into the first stitch),
> *Once around the back* (wrapping the yarn around the right needle at the back of the work),
> *Peek through the window* (pulling the wrapped yarn toward the front, through the stitch),
> *Off jumps Jack* (pulling the new stitch up and off the left needle).

ENCOURAGE THEM

Always tell new knitters how well they are doing so that their interest doesn't wane. Even if their first knitting is misshapen and riddled with holes, find something positive to say to keep them going. And remember to keep that first sample so that they can look back later and see how much they have progressed.

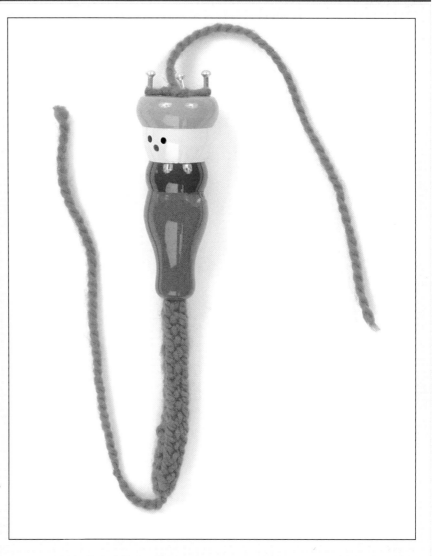

chapter

Happy Endings

Congratulations! You have embarked on a richly satisfying lifetime hobby that is both relaxing and productive. There is nothing like the sense of accomplishment and pride you feel upon completing a knitting project. Be sure to share your hobby with others; knitting friends are the best kind. This final chapter covers a few tips for organizing your knitting and also provides some useful knitting resources.

Managing Your Yarn

You have probably heard seasoned knitters talk about their yarn stashes. Some knitters have so much yarn that it would take years to knit it all. You, too, may come to acquire quite an array of yarns and tools; or you may start one project, put it aside to start another, and end up with a collection of unfinished projects. That's why it's a good idea to get a handle on how to manage your knitting.

STORING YARN

If you're going to put yarn away for any length of time, it's a good idea to store it in a dry, dust-free, mothproof environment. You should use cedar blocks to keep the moths away, and you should try to keep the yarn fresh in a plastic storage bin or zipped sweater bag. Zipper-type bags work well for small amounts of yarn.

STORING UNFINISHED PROJECTS

If you have to put an unfinished project on hold, it's a good idea to store it the same way you store yarn long term. You should put in a cedar block; it would be very upsetting to find that moths had gotten in and spoiled your hard work. You should also tuck in a note that indicates where you are in the pattern, any changes to the pattern you might have made, and any special notes or reminders having to do with your instructions. You would be surprised how much you can forget in just a couple months!

LEFTOVER YARN?

After you have completed several projects, you will find that you're starting a collection of leftover yarn. Save all your odds and ends and use them for contrast pompoms or tassels on hats, or twist them together to form your own tweed yarn. If you want to practice various stitch patterns, these leftovers will certainly come in handy. And cotton leftovers make great dishrags and baby washcloths.

REJUVENATING USED YARN

Sometimes you may have to unravel your work and start over, or you may decide to unravel an out-of-date fashion and re-knit it into something else. You can rejuvenate that kinky unraveled yarn. Simply wind it into a loose hank, soak it in sudsy lukewarm water, rinse well, and hang the hank to dry. When it's dry, you can wind the yarn loosely into a ball.

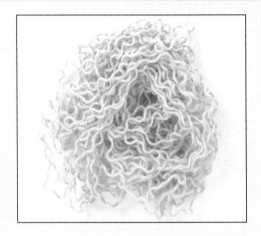

KEEPING TRACK OF YOUR NEEDLES

At some point, you may find yourself in a yarn shop choosing materials for a new project but not remembering if you already have the appropriate needles at home. Why not keep a record of what needles you have on a small card in your wallet? That way you won't end up with too many duplicates. By the same token, you may want to keep on hand a wish list of materials needed for projects you want to make in the future. You never know when you might come across the perfect yarn.

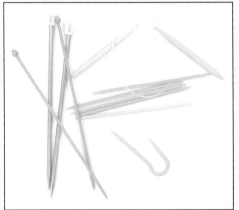

TIP

Finding a New Home for Old Yarn

If you're like most knitters, eventually your stash gets so big that you know you'll never use some of it. And if your tastes change, you may no longer love that yarn you just had to have a decade ago. A fun way to get rid of part of your stash is to invite your knitting friends for a stash giveaway. You win because you reduce the size of your stash, and your friends win because they get new and exciting yarns for free. A stash trade is fun, too, but of course it means you're adding more yarn to your own stash!

Looking Again at Gauge

Of all the things you have learned about knitting, gauge is one of the most important and most overlooked concepts. Though gauge is already covered in Chapter 6, too much emphasis cannot be placed on achieving the proper gauge before beginning a project. All designs begin with a gauge swatch. Every measurement and every bit of shaping relies on the specified gauge.

PROVING THE POINT ABOUT GAUGE

Here is a scenario that should prove how important it is to knit to the exact gauge of your knitting pattern. Say you are knitting a hat that should have a finished brim circumference of 20 inches. Your pattern calls for a gauge of 3 stitches per inch and therefore asks you to cast on 60 stitches. You make a gauge swatch and find that you are getting a gauge of 2½ stitches per inch. You figure that a half-stitch difference is close enough and proceed with the knitting of the hat. When you finish the hat, you find that it is far too big, that the brim is actually 24 inches around. That's because 60 stitches divided by 2½ equals 24. A mere half stitch can add up to a big difference when multiplied over many stitches. You would not want to spend weeks working on a sweater in an expensive yarn only to find that in the end it is much too small.

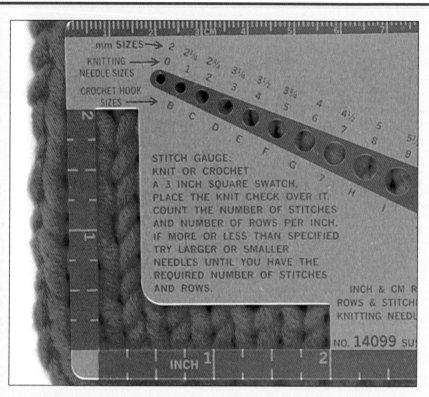

THE ILLUSIVE ROW GAUGE

While it is of utmost importance to attain an accurate stitch gauge, it is not always easy to attain both the stitch and row gauge that your pattern calls for. While row gauge is not always as crucial as stitch gauge—because many patterns call for you to knit something until it is a certain number of inches long rather than for calling you to knit a specified number of rows—there are many instances in which you may have to make adjustments to make up for inaccurate row gauge. Say you are knitting a striped hat, and the pattern says to knit a certain number of rows per stripe and to complete a certain number of stripes before shaping the top. If you are getting less length per row than the pattern specifies, then you will have to knit more rows per stripe or knit more stripes than the pattern calls for to achieve the correct length before shaping the top.

If you are a diligent knitter who always makes a gauge swatch before starting a project, you will end up with quite a collection of interesting little squares. Don't throw them away because there are many things you can do with these swatches.

THE KNITTING PROJECT DIARY

Some knitters like to keep a diary or scrapbook of the projects they have completed. Putting your gauge swatch, along with notes about and photos of the project, into a scrapbook can be a useful resource to look back on when working on new projects. Keeping such a record will also track your progress as a knitter.

SWATCH PROJECTS

You can sew swatches together to make a colorful throw or a doll blanket. Or why not sew two squares together to make a bean bag? Six 4-inch swatches makes a set of three colorful bean bags for juggling. Four 4-inch swatches knit in cotton make a unique washcloth. Perhaps thinking of fun gauge swatch projects will provide the impetus to knit a swatch before beginning every bigger project.

Appendix

Reference Materials

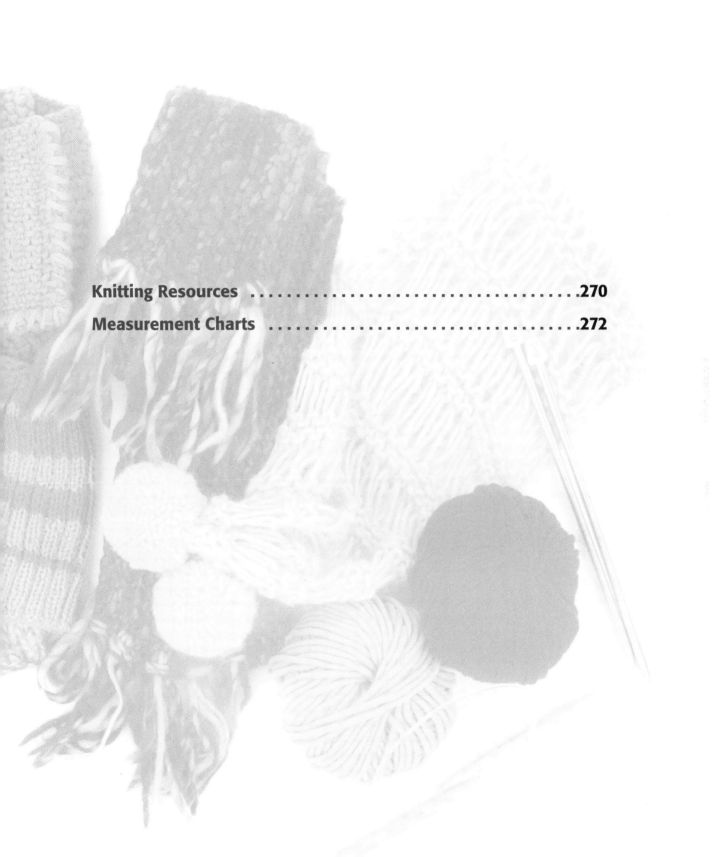

Knitting Resources

By now you are becoming an avid knitter, and you want to find out more about where to get yarn and tools. Or perhaps you want to join a knitting guild. This appendix tells you where you can find yarn- and knitting-related information.

YOUR LOCAL YARN SHOP

It's a good idea to establish a relationship with your local yarn shop (or LYS, as seasoned knitters call it), if you're fortunate enough to have one. Shopping for yarn in person is always the best method because you can see the actual colors and touch the yarns. Your local yarn shop owner and employees can also help with technical questions, yarn substitutions, pattern selection, and much more. You can find a list of yarn shops online at www.woolworks.org/stores.html.

KNITTING GUILDS

If you're really enthusiastic, you can join your local knitting guild. Knitting guilds usually meet once a month, and they also sponsor various knitting events. Yarn markets, knitting conventions, design contests, fashion shows, knitting lunches, and lectures by knitwear designers are all knitting-related events that you may gain access to through joining a knitting guild. You can also join The Knitting Guild Association (TKGA), a national guild. Visit its Web site, at www.tkga.com. Or you can look for a guild near you at www.woolworks.org/guilds.html, where local knitting guilds are listed by state.

KNITTING MAGAZINES

The selection of knitting magazines available has grown over the years. These are a few of the most popular knitting magazines:

Cast On   *Knit.1*
Family Circle Easy Knitting   *Knit 'n Style*
Interweave Knits   *Vogue Knitting*
Knitter's Magazine

A few yarn companies also put out magazines, which are actually pattern support for their yarns. You can subscribe to these magazines so that you receive them as soon as they come out. A couple of these are:

Rebecca (GGH/Muench Yarns)   *Rowan Magazine* (Rowan Yarns)

KNITTING RESOURCES ON THE INTERNET

There is a wealth of knitting information on the Internet. Some online magazines are:

www.knitty.com
www.knitnet.com
www.knittersreview.com

www.magknits.com
www.spunmag.com
www.knittinguniverse.com

There are also a lot of Web sites that offer free patterns, knitting instruction, yarn shop listings, product reviews, and other information. A few good knitting information sites are:

www.woolworks.com
www.knitting.about.com
www.sweaterbabe.com

www.craftyarncouncil.com
www.learntoknit.com
www.fibergypsy.com

There are numerous Internet-only suppliers, and many yarn shops also maintain Web sites from which you can purchase supplies. A few of these are:

www.elann.com
www.knitpicks.com
www.patternworks.com
www.nobleknits.com

www.knittingzone.com
www.knittingbag.com
www.yarn.com
www.yarnmarket.com

You can also find free patterns, as well as knitters' blogs and chat rooms, all over the Internet.

Measurement Charts

Included here are measurement charts for infants (sizes 3 to 24 months), children (sizes 2 to 16), women (sizes X-Small to 5X), and men (sizes Small to XX-Large). We've also included a head circumference measurement chart, which covers infants (preemies, babies, and toddlers), children, and adults (both women and men). Measurements are given in both inches and centimeters. For more information about standard measurements, check out the Web site www.yarnstandards.com from the Craft Yarn Council of America.

Babies' Sizes					
Baby's Size (not age):	**3 months**	**6 months**	**12 months**	**18 months**	**24 months**
Chest					
Inches	16	17	18	19	20
Centimeters	40.5	43	45.5	48	50.5
Center Back Neck-to-Cuff					
Inches	10½	11½	12½	14	18
Centimeters	26.5	29	31.5	35.5	45.5
Back Waist Length					
Inches	6	7	7½	8	8½
Centimeters	15.5	17.5	19	20.5	21.5
Across Back (Shoulder to Shoulder)					
Inches	7¼	7¾	8¼	8½	8¾
Centimeters	18.5	19.5	21	21.5	22
Sleeve Length to Underarm					
Inches	6	6½	7½	8	8½
Centimeters	15.5	16.5	19	20.5	21.5

Children's Sizes								
Size	**2**	**4**	**6**	**8**	**10**	**12**	**14**	**16**
Chest								
Inches	21	23	25	26½	28	30	31½	32½
Centimeters	53	58.5	63.5	67	71	76	80	82.5
Center Back Neck-to-Cuff								
Inches	18	19½	20½	22	24	26	27	28
Centimeters	45.5	49.5	52	56	61	66	68.5	71
Back Waist Length								
Inches	8½	9½	10½	12½	14	15	15½	16
Centimeters	21.5	24	26.5	31.5	35.5	38	39.5	40.5
Across Back (Shoulder to Shoulder)								
Inches	9¼	9¾	10¼	10¾	11¼	12	12¼	13
Centimeters	23.5	25	26	27	28.5	30.5	31	33
Sleeve Length to Underarm								
Inches	8½	10½	11½	12½	13½	15	16	16½
Centimeters	21.5	26.5	29	31.5	34.5	38	40.5	42

Measurement
Charts (continued)

Women's Sizes									
Size	X-Small	Small	Medium	Large	1X	2X	3X	4X	5X
Bust									
Inches	28–30	32–34	36–38	40–42	44–46	48–50	52–54	56–58	60–62
Centimeters	71–76	81–86	91.5–96.5	101.5–106.5	111.5–117	122–127	132–137	142–147	152–158
Center Back Neck-to-Cuff									
Inches	27–27½	28–28½	29–29½	30–30½	31–31½	31½–32	32½–33	32½–33	33–33½
Centimeters	68.5–70	71–72.5	73.5–75	76–77.5	78.5–80	80–81.5	82.5–84	82.5–84	84–85
Back Waist Length									
Inches	16½	17	17¼	17½	17¾	18	18	18½	18½
Centimeters	42	43	43.5	44.5	45	45.5	45.5	47	47
Across Back (Shoulder to Shoulder)									
Inches	14–14½	14½–15	16–16½	17–17½	17½	18	18	18½	18½
Centimeters	35.5–37	37–38	40.5–42	43–44.5	44.5	44.5	45.5	47	47
Sleeve Length to Underarm									
Inches	16½	17	17	17½	17½	18	18	18½	18½
Centimeters	42	43	43	44.5	44.5	45.5	45.5	47	47

Men's Sizes					
Size	*Small*	*Medium*	*Large*	*X-Large*	*XX-Large*
Chest					
Inches	34–36	38–40	42–44	46–48	50–52
Centimeters	86–91.5	96.5–101.5	106.5–111.5	116.5–122	127–132
Center Back Neck-to-Cuff					
Inches	32–32½	33–33½	34–34½	35–35½	36–36½
Centimeters	81–82.5	83.5–85	86.5–87.5	89–90	91.5–92.5
Back Hip Length					
Inches	25–25½	26½–26¾	27–27¼	27½–27¾	28–28½
Centimeters	63.5–64.5	67.5–68	68.5–69	69.5–70.5	71–72.5
Across Back (Shoulder to Shoulder)					
Inches	15½–16	16½–17	17½–18	18–18½	18½–19
Centimeters	39.5–40.5	42–43	44.5–45.5	45.5–47	47–48
Sleeve Length to Underarm					
Inches	18	18½	19½	20	20½
Centimeters	45.5	47	49.5	50.5	52

Head Circumference					
	Infant/Child				Adult
	Preemie	*Baby*	*Toddler*	*Child*	*Woman*	*Man*
Inches	12	14	16	18	20	22
Centimeters	30.5	35.5	40.5	45.5	50.5	56

Index

D

dbl (double, crochet), 80
dc (double cross), 80
dec (decreases, decreasing), 80
decorative details
    beads, 198–199
    borders, 197
    edge crocheting, 192–195
    embroidery stitches, 188–191
    fringe, 184–185
    pompoms, 178–181
    ruffles, 196
    tassels, 182–183
    tubular cords, 186
    twisted cords, 187
decrease 1, shaping techniques, 54–57
decrease multiple stitches, shaping techniques, 58–59
diag (diagonal), 80
diagonal check pattern stitch, complicated knit and purl pattern, 43
diagonal lace, knitting technique, 113
diagonal rib stitch, rib pattern, 41
diam (diameter), 80
diameter (shaft), needle sizing measurement, 10
diamond brocade pattern stitch, complicated knit and purl pattern, 44
diamonds in columns stitch, complicated knit and purl pattern, 44
diary, knitting project, 267
DK (double knitting), 7, 80
double asterisk (**), separate instructions, 81
double bar increase, shaping technique, 52
double cable (12-stitch panel), stitch pattern, 101
double decrease, shaping technique, 58
double knitting (DK), 7, 80
double make one increase, shaping technique, 52
double-pointed needles
    cast-on techniques, 92
    circular knitting techniques, 93
    needle shape type, 11
double seed stitch, simple pattern, 36
double vertical decrease, shaping technique, 59
double yarn over increase, shaping technique, 52
dpn (double-pointed needle), 80
dropped stitches, correction techniques, 68–71
dropped stitch scarf, easy knitting project, 213–214
drop stitches, knitting technique, 108
drop stitch garter pattern, knitting technique, 108
dtr (double treble, crochet), 80
duplicate stitch, embroidery technique, 189
dye lot numbers, label information element, 8

E

easy horizontal scarf, easy knitting project, 202–203
easy pointed border, knitting technique, 197
edge stitches, dropped stitch correction technique, 71
embroidery stitches, 188–191
ending with an RS row, defined, 82
ending with a WS row, defined, 82
English method
    knitting technique, 20–21
    needle and yarn holding technique, 18
    purl technique, 24–25
epi (ends per inch), 80
every other row, defined, 82
eyelet chevrons, knitting technique, 110
eyelet patterns, knitting technique, 110–111

F

Fair Isle knitting, color knitting technique, 120–123
falling rain pattern, knitting technique, 111
fastener (button), selection guidelines, 166–167
fasten off, defined, 82
FC (front cross), 80
felting, described, 179
fiber content, label information element, 8
fingering (baby), yarn weight classification, 7
finger knitting, 260–261
finishing details
    blocking techniques, 138–139
    button bands, 156
    button (fastener) selection guidelines, 166–167
    buttonhole reinforcement, 164–165
    buttonholes, 158–163
    button sewing, 168–169
    collars, 157
    grafting, 144–147
    knit in hems, 175
    neckbands, 156
    picking up stitches, 152–155
    plackets, 156
    pockets, 170–173
    seam sewing, 140–143
    turned hems, 174
    weave in ends, 136–137
foll (follows, following), 80
French knots, embroidery technique, 191
fringe, 184–185
from beg, defined, 82
front cross cable, stitch pattern, 99